Forgotten Women
A Tribute in Poetry

for Sandy —
never forgotten! —
♡ Laura

Forgotten Women
A Tribute in Poetry

edited by Ginny Lowe Connors
with an Introduction by Marilyn Kallet

GRAYSON BOOKS
WEST HARTFORD, CT
www.GraysonBooks.com

Forgotten Women: A Tribute in Poetry
Copyright © 2017 by Ginny Connors
ISBN: 978-0-9962809-9-0
Published by Grayson Books
West Hartford, Connecticut
Printed in the USA

    Forgotten women (Connors)
      Forgotten women : a tribute in poetry / edited by
    Ginny Lowe Connors.
      pages cm
      Includes bibliographical references and index.
      ISBN 978-0-9962809-9-0

      1. Women--Poetry. 2. American poetry--Women authors.
    3. Poetry.   I. Connors, Ginny Lowe, editor.
    II. Title.

    PS595.W59F67 2016   811.008'03522
                      QBI16-900045

Interior & Cover Design: Cindy Mercier

Cover Art: A Dark Pool c.1908, © Reproduced with permission of The Estate of Dame Laura Knight DBE RA 2017. All Rights Reserved

GraysonBooks.com

After all, Ginger Rogers did everything that Fred Astaire did.
She just did it backwards and in high heels.

Ann Richards

Contents

In the Shadows of Their Men

Making Herstory

Introduction

"Time is male," Adrienne Rich wrote, in her poem "Snapshots of a Daughter in Law," found in the book by that same title, 1963. Rich was meditating on and debunking the idea of uninterrupted transcendental time, rejecting gendered ideology. Rich is no longer with us, alas, but the generous volume in hand, *Forgotten Women*, edited by Ginny Lowe Connors, continues the feminist work of documenting and imagining women's achievements. Silences, invisibility, undervaluing, can be at least partially undone by volumes such as this one. The book illumines herstory and the present by focusing on images of women and on women's words. This anthology raises our spirits and literary intelligence, as we meet historical women of art, science, and literature—famous women re-evaluated imaginatively—and glimpse those working behind the scenes who never had a chance to be known or celebrated. *Forgotten Women* gathers poems by and about extraordinary women of accomplishment and ordinary women who juggled too many demands, women whose work was overshadowed by male colleagues or famous husbands, women rendered invisible until now.

The first section of this volume, "Hard Work," covers a topic we find too little of in literature: work, the narrative of the working lives of women and men, whether we are factory workers or teachers, housekeepers, astronomers, seamstresses, single mothers. Images of women working are particularly underrepresented in literary works. It has been more than forty years since Tillie Olsen published the first edition of *Silences*, her study and critique of how and why writers—particularly women writers—were stymied in their creative lives by the necessities of work and by patriarchal critics, editors and publishers. She reminded us that artists and writers need uninterrupted time for their best work: "Wholly surrendered and dedicated lives; time as needed for the work; totality of self. But women are traditionally trained to place others' needs first..." (*Silences*, 1979 ed., 17.)

In "Hard Work" we learn the names of workers like Emily Fish, a lighthouse keeper ("A Light Keeper's Words to Her Husband," Denise Utt); Sarah Stone, natural history illustrator ("Sarah Stone Paints the O'o Bird, 1973, Lever Museum," Sherry Rind); and Rosalind Franklin, who worked in the laboratory where the double helix DNA was discovered and explained to the world ("I Award My Own Nobel Prize to Rosalind Franklin," Allison Thorpe). Vivian Shipley's extended poem in finely crafted tercets, "The Radium Girls," offers a lyrical history of those who worked with radium and paid a mortal price; this well-wrought poem is worth the price of admission to this book. These are just a few of the heroines—the vital history lessons—we absorb through the beautiful work of this section.

"Unknown to the World, the World to Someone," the second section of this anthology, offers intimate portraits of women at home, women in domestic life, immigrant women and those who made new homes for their families. This section sets before us images of women who suffered in the fields and deserts and somehow managed to keep going. As Paula Sergi writes in "Sherpa," "Someone has to haul / all our crap up hill…"

Not all of the poems in this section or in this book are by women. Joseph Bathanti's "Women's Prison," depicting inmates in their "girlish rawboned glory," keeps company with poetry by former Poet Laureate Ted Kooser. The theme of work crosses over into this section, too, as we read about "Lessons" by Jennifer Freed, and observe an immigrant woman trying to absorb the subtleties of verb tenses from her tutor.

The third section, "In the Shadows of Their Men," fascinates us with imagined narratives from wives, friends, daughters of notable men, artists and scientists among them. At last we hear from Fanny Mendelssohn, the sister of Felix, in a gorgeous, richly textured poem by Christine Casson, "Programme Music"; from Pauline Bonaparte, Napoleon's sister, in a prose poem by Lynn Schmeidler, "Of Unforgettable." One poem that stands out in this artful chapter is "Monique Braille's Confession," by Susan J. Erickson, where Louis Braille's mother declares: "I am not a wheel on the carriage / that takes Louis away, nor the ridged / track left in the mud. I am the patched /elbow of the republic of motherhood." What a killer last line! This section and the entire book are rife with memorable lines.

The last section in this remarkable anthology, "Making Herstory," takes us through an impressive sampler of poems about women who changed history in notable public ways, and in underreported actions. The poetic journey begins with Virginia Dare, and travels to Annie Oakley, and to heroic Claudette Colvin, who preceded Rosa Parks by refusing to go to the back of the bus: "before Rosa she saw the way, / she was the way" ("Montgomery Bus Arrest, March 2, 1955," Laura Altshul). The narrative arc of the book takes a global turn, in poetry about women miners in South Africa, longed-for women's friendships in Gaza, a nameless woman seen in a Polish photograph—nameless but not forgotten in Elaine Zimmerman's understated and moving poem, "Photo in Krakow." The poet declares, "It is never too late to / honor the dead and pray for the living."

Women divers, women climbers, women pioneer pilots: the book's reach extends to heaven, hell, earth, and the seas, through the eyes and dreams of the skilled poets assembled within its covers. This rich collection should serve Women's Studies and literature programs well.

Individual readers will likely keep this book on their nightstands for company, and carry it in their backpacks for courage and inspiration. A large volume, yes, but its pages suggest to the reader that there is more digging and uncovering of notable and courageous women still to be done by all of us who value women's work. *Forgotten Women* are no longer forgotten when the reader participates with the poets by listening, engaging with the stories we were never taught, the necessary stories of women who paved the way, "who were the way."

Dr. Marilyn Kallet
Nancy Moore Goslee Professor of English, University of Tennessee

Hard Work

Why She Wasn't Invited to Join the Geological Society of London

Jeanne Wagner

At first, she hunts only with her father, finds fossils the way
a poor person finds things,

looks for the random glint of a penny in the gutter, the wink
of its coppery shine.

At daybreak, she goes out with him wanting to see a day
spilling its light on sand,

but finds the sea's wildness instead, finds the wind making
a bonnet of her hair;

finds the basket on her arm full of what the Black Ven holds
out for her.

And because she sells what she finds as trinkets to tourists,
peddles them

in the open, the way a woman might sell her own beauty
to a willing buyer,

or the way a gypsy might hawk her charms, calling them
snake-stones, devil's fingers,

calling them common names; a common woman, half-
educated, unmarried,

with coarse hands, wind-licked hag-hair, hems savaged
by sea salt.

Because sometimes when she releases a skeleton from
its stratum of limestone and shale,

she feels more of a midwife than a scholar; she thinks
of her favorites,

the ammonites, spherical, fetal, curving into themselves
like stillborn things.

Because sometimes she unearths monsters: chimera,
griffins and basilisks,

bodies unbiblical, unsanctified, otherworldly, unholy.
She keeps them in her parlor,

their ungainly necks, their beaks, the long bony fingers
reaching for flight.

*Mary Anning (1799–1847) was a British fossil collector and dealer who,
though often ignored professionally, became known around the world for
important finds, including ichthyosaurs, plesiosaurs and pterosaurs.*

My First Rescue

Suellen Wedmore

On that September day I spied
   the pitching catboat, heard the laughter—

four about my age, sixteen, sons
   of Newport's finest, I guessed,

judging by the boat, the sleek and shiny
   Hug-Em-Snug—all hooting, wrestling,

then one of them, waving his arms
   & suddenly shimmying up the mast

so that, top heavy, it plunged
   into the churning sea & the boat

took on water until the hull
   rolled toward sky, dumping all

the young men into the cold
   & choppy Atlantic, the upturned hull

slippery, frigid, so small only two
   could grasp it, the others treading water,

gasping, all screaming *Help!*

I jumped into my skiff, rowed
   hard & fast across the surf

until, beside them, I stabilized
   my boat with one oar,

& drew them, like Pa had taught,
   one by one, across the stern

into the skiff, & hauled back
   to the island, to fireplace,

blankets, Mama's molasses toddies—
one of them, tall & hazel-eyed

Samuel Powell unconscious,
but once revived grabbed my hand,

shook it until it hurt & gushed
thankyouthankyouthankyou

and yet on the mainland, it would be
eleven years—when the Evening News

proclaimed me heroine for a day—
that he admitted to his family

it was a mere keeper's daughter
who'd saved his lucky life.

Ida (Idawalley Zorada) Lewis was 15 years old in 1857 when her family moved to Lime Rock Light, off the coast of Newport, Rhode Island, where her father had been appointed keeper. When her father suffered a stroke, Ida and her mother tended the light together. After her father's death, her mother became ill and it was Ida alone who maintained the Light Station. She is reported to have saved between 18 and 36 lives during her 54 years as unofficial and official keeper of Lime Rock Light.

A Light Keeper's Words to Her Husband

Denise Utt

I would have come sooner
but that nightfall the waves rose like sharks
tossing a ship limp and, with the fog
too thick for the light to cut, I knew
that if the bay's rocky jaw bit into that ship,
I'd be fishing men up. The fog signal choked
and so I hammered her metal. My arm,
lame as a broken wave, but I kept pounding.
I got through those hours knowing you
were with me. Like I felt you with me in '06,
the sun but a thumbnail's rim, when the quake
rocked the tower and I fought the fire
that bullied the flame in the lantern's belly.

People tell me I'll turn cloudy, anchored
so far from town, but I've got the horses,
poodles, chickens and cows, and my light
that make a mother proud. The house,
dressed in antiques and fine china, is ready
for whenever the naval officers and artists tidal in.
And now, leaves that idle in the wind
alight on your stone. Their hands rustle
and I hear the wind whisper,
There's not enough time to be lonely.

*Emily Fish was an early woman keeper of the 1855 Point Pinos lighthouse for
Monterey Bay whose primary job was to maintain the lamp. She was notable
not only for her competence as keeper, but for the socialite life she had known
and that she brought to the Monterey Bay lighthouse from 1893-1914, mixing
fashionable dinner parties with long, physically demanding days and nights.*

Sarah Stone Paints the O'o Bird, 1783, Lever Museum

Sherry Rind

From Cook's Hawaiian plunder
Miss Stone extracts a red and gold cape,
sketches the folds, hints
at the eighty thousand birds
plucked for a king.

In her hands, shadow's the illusion
of lift and heft, a feather's weightlessness;
color's the clue to every mystery—
how a touch of moss brightens the red
and the hidden gold
of an olive-brown bird becomes a cloak.

Below, she replicates the tattered specimen.
She adds a white hair-stroke along the iris
suggesting the infinite patience of animals
who know their fate. The O'o's beak points
to the cloak, its eye at the families
strolling through the short-lived museum.

The cloak whispers as the feathers shift
against each other, simulation
of a bird lifting and ruffling its feathers
to hook a million tiny barbs into place.
Miss Stone smooths the page before the long sleep.

Sarah Stone, 1760-1844, was a natural history illustrator who painted specimens brought to the Lever Museum from all over the world, particularly from Captain Cook's voyages. The museum and much of her work was dispersed in 1806 and few of her paintings are available for public view.

Belly-Ache Bush with Giant Sphinx Moth: Plate #15 by Maria Sibylla Merian

Carol Berg

This is what I mean by a riot of openings:
five-petal leaves grow dripping
bones from the center vine. The caterpillar eats
the east of each leaf like a koan, cracking them
into fields of reasonable inches.

At least I see them as bones the way they rattle in this surveying wind.

This is what I mean by the ocher cracks open:
my life is a test here I snag my mind upon.
The process of thinking a chrysalis a pushing through.
Are my fingers my paints a crackling fire?
What reason withholds my center?

Or do I mean centering. This is what I mean
by a wide-open concern: The Giant Sphinx
Moth with its curves of tongues.
Once the feathers were only a private inside.
Once the words inside me were captive, cocooned.

Maria Sibylla Merian was an entomologist in the 1700s who traveled by herself to Surinam to do research and to make gorgeous plates of the insects in all their various stages.

Laura Knight, Self-Portrait, 1913

Kathleen McClung

"How holy is the human body when bare of other than the sun."
        —Laura Knight, The Magic of a Line, 1965

My legacy? Hmm. My sketchbooks—penciled nudes—
will not survive the Cornwall damp. Each page
will gum and stink of mildew. Platitudes,
as well, will curdle for some years: *Outrage!*
Indecent! How dare she? Yet I must dare
to paint my self, hair tucked inside black hat,
my face in profile, gazing at her bare
and holy body—Ella, friend, palms at
her skull, feet steady on striped cloth, her spine
unclothed, unbent. My model will not live
as long as I. She will not praise light nine
decades, mourn two world wars. But we will give
beyond this red of sweater, cream and pink
of skin. What lasts? Discovering, I think.

Painter Laura Knight (1877-1970) shattered centuries-old taboos facing
women artists. Working with a live model, she represented a nude woman in
her self-portrait: Knight's friend and fellow artist Ella Naper.

Alice Neel, Nude Self-Portrait, 1980

Kathleen McClung

Dear Alice, kin, what lasts? Your daughters die.
Firstborn, diphtheria, the second, suicide.
One lover slashes fifty canvases, and I
admit even this sonnet strays, threatens to hide
in idly Googling sites that document
desertions, opium, shoplifting food.
Bouquets, but questions for you, Alice, shoulders bent
at 80, glasses crooked, Mother Hubbard nude
on blue striped chair, your irises this shade
of azure too. I cheer your nakedness
and try to read your face. Have you conveyed
some wisdom of the very old? Or wariness
may simply be your signature. Each face
you paint—not quite alarmed, just shy of grace.

Alice Neel (1900-1984), like Laura Knight before her, broke centuries-old taboos facing women artists. She represented a nude woman in her self-portrait: herself at the age of 80.

The Radium Girls

Vivian Shipley

I. February 1, 2004: Mae Keane, 97, Speaks to Men Cleaning Enterprise Apartment 507, Waterbury, CT

Wear white lab coats, plastic masks and rubber gloves
while you vacuum radioactive dust from wooden floors,
scrape then scrub radium from the ceiling and walls,

but you will still inhale my history. This Cherry Street
room was a radium dial studio from 1919 to 1927.
Waterbury Clock Company owners dressed like you

inspected this room, knew radium could kill me
and my 17 girlfriends who died with bones crumbling,
jaws rotting. 1926. I had just turned 19, thought painting

glow-in-the dark watch faces would be respectable.
Paid 8 cents a dial, my boss said work faster, sharpen
bristles with my lips. Lippointing bitter taste of radium

made me gag. The day I made 62 cents, he growled,
find another job. I wanted to trample dials underfoot,
let him know I was on the way to better things, but I

was dazed, a toad. To breathe clean air, take a break,
go to Timexpo Museum just a few yards away. Sure,
you'll see 150 years of timepieces, Timex's *torture test*

commercials, but you won't find a word about us,
the Radium Girls. Timex never has admitted we're part
of its history. Out front is a 40 foot Easter Island statue

but no black marble monument chiseled with birth
and death dates for girls whose futures contracted, who
dreamed in past tense: Elizabeth Dunn, Marjorie Domschott,

Louise Pine, Mildred Cardow, Marion Demolis, Helen Wall,
Ann Mullenite, Ethel Daniels, Edith Lapiana, Mabel Adkins,
and Florence Koss. Statistics, their sores did not heal,

their tongues were not freed. Canaries in the coal mine,
song in their throat was a prayer their deaths would save
others. Memory, more bitter than radium that tunneled

into their hearts, is in this room's walls you are disturbing.
Awakened, voices of girls who worked here are not erased,
will not be stilled any longer. They are filtering through.

II. Frances Splettstocher, 21

February, 1925, first dial painter to die in Waterbury, I had
lippointed for 4 years, did think it strange that my handkerchief
glowed in the dark when I blew my nose, but church members,

makers of Waterbury's Dollar Watches, wouldn't let young girls
like us do anything harmful. First I mixed glue, water, radium
powder to make glowing greenish-white paint, then applied it

with a camel hair brush to dial numbers. A few strokes, brushes
lost their shape and I couldn't paint accurately. My teacher told
me to point the brush with my lips. I did this about six times for

every watch dial. The paint didn't taste funny—it didn't have
taste. Next to me racks of altimeters and clock dials waited
like upturned faces of children I would never have. I was

proud of Marie Curie who won two Nobel Prizes for discovering
liquid sunshine. How could I know it would be my embalming
fluid or that in 1922, Amelia Maggia died in Orange, NJ,

jawbone so rotten that the dentist lifted her entire mandible out
of her mouth. US Radium recorded cause of death as *syphilis*,
didn't mention chemists used lead screens, masks and tongs

to handle radium while Amelia sucked in death. My friend Elsie
told me not to have a tooth pulled but in February,1925, I did.
The hole in my cheek would not heal; my uncle would pay

me a dime to go away so he did not have to look at it.
At least I wasn't like Katherine Moore who slapped radium
around like it was cake frosting. With a grapefruit size tumor

jutting from her chin, her jaw was so deformed she didn't go
out in public without pulling her coat collar up. My family
worked in the clock factory, my father had *spelter shakes*,

my uncle *metal fume fever*, my brother *brass founder's ague*.
Quailing, my father was sure radium poisoning was killing me;
he dared not make any kick about it because he'd lose his job.

My own words dogpaddled, even when I listened to my heart,
cold disc of stethoscope on my chest, blood punching chambers
like fists in kid gloves nice girls like me wore in the 1920s.

III. Edna Steberet, 35

Only 21, my friend Frances went to a better place with no
numbers to paint for men with hearts that beat like wind up
watches that ticked off her days. I still remember her standing,

one foot behind the other calf, rubbing her shoe on seam
of her silk stocking. It was the publicity, not her death,
that caused Waterbury Clock company to officially ban

lippointing, but not the use of radium. For a time our boss
gave us bowls of water to rinse brushes before putting
them in our mouth. Hard to keep water clean, we wasted

too much time and paint, and he took away the bowls.
I never stopped wetting my brush with my lips—I wanted
money for clothes to attract a special guy. Cobbling a life

together, I knew watches I painted were going to troops
overseas. I scratched my name and address on the back of dials.
Lots of GIs were lonely and wrote to me. I hoped a soldier

or sailor would visit, find me all dolled up, my hair rolled
into finger curls, pink silk dress, feet skewered into patent
high heels, hose without runs. I was young, filled with life.

Was it so wrong to want fun? After work, I was covered
with luminous powder, my clothes, fingers glowed, hair
shone in the dark. Some nights, I'd invite neighborhood kids

to come over to play *watch Edna glow* in a closet. First, there
were holes for my tongue to probe; at the end, I'd lost all
my teeth, could not sit up or walk. No man wanted me then.

In summer, positioned on the front porch, if I sat facing road,
I wanted company, sidewise profile to the street, friends could
say hello, my back to the road, I was in my housecoat, hair

uncombed. Night swallowed my voice. Needing to fool
my weary heart, like wise men going to Bethlehem, I searched
sky for a word, for a star to guide me to what would come next.

IV. Margaret O'Brien, 39

Proud that at 15 I could earn up to $24 a week compared
to $5 anywhere else, I was also learning a decent trade. Long
dusty tables were in this room you are cleaning. Air was stale,

hot as a kiln, motion baked out. Vain, I wore a shirtwaist
and skirt, had bobbed hair because I liked the night life.
After work I played the piano or like a packrat, I organized

my hope chest just like penny poppy shows I had put on
as a girl—I saved odd things, a cork from Portuguese port,
snake skull, piece of blue sea glass. I dug a hole in ground,

lined it with shards of broken mirror around my treasures,
then covered it with a piece of cardboard. Boys had to pay,
a caramel, a penny to see my show for a minute. Pop it open,

pop it shut. Even then, boys said I was delicious with lashes
dipping onto freckled cheeks. My high school year book
labeled me Peg. Soft-spoken, I was a bookworm, prone to

giggling fits in the library. Around Halloween, to take
a break from working, have a laugh, the other girls and I
would paint our face and turn off lights in this Cherry Street

room. It was playfulness that killed us, what we put between
our lips without knowing. My boss told me, *Not to worry.*
If you swallow any radium, it'll make your cheeks rosy.

I had a good time while I could, was a hit on St. Patrick's Day
when I painted my buttons, nails and teeth with green radium
to surprise my boyfriend. Then, the doctor's stethoscope

vined my back. Breathe. Breathe, he said, trying to teach
me how I could live on will, on desire. Biting back panic,
how could I pray for inner peace? I couldn't control my heart.

Even though I was tempted, I never drank like my father,
head tipped for amber to numb my throat, kitchen chair
wedged under a doorknob so I would not be surprised.

V. Josephine Pascucci Lamb, 79

One brief burst of blood into air and I'll be free. 1974.
In and out of bed for 50 years, I went blind at 24 before
I set eyes on my only child, William. I knew I was a beauty—

wavy onyx hair, Italian complexion. I don't know if the color
of my eyes changed from brown to opal. Delicate fingers,
still it was not easy to paint tiny numbers on watches. I was

quick, didn't earn enough to pay for college but could buy
a silk dress and shoes each week. That's how I caught the eye
of Will's father—he left when our son was 5. I can't blame

him. What man wants to be a nurse? My sorrow did not stop
the leaves. At first, I lumbered through, tried to wear down
the clock, prayed to be released, for sound to leave my body.

My mother taught me I was here to wait for death, pleasures
of earth which she never discussed were overrated. Why try
to be stouthearted? My answer—to make sweet memories

for my Will. The iceman had a wooden truck lined with zinc.
Snow rained as he sawed blocks of ice. I taught Will to cup
his hands to catch it, then run home where I'd put vanilla,

lemon extract, grenadine, or molasses on it. Son unlike father,
Will has read me the *Waterbury American* each day so I
could check off names in obituaries of 16 girls I worked side

by side with in this room you are cleaning. Can't you hear
voices bumping like bats at these windows? Waterbury Clock
compensated 16 of us for illness or our families for death,

promised free medical care. Even though the president never
admitted I was maimed by radium poisoning, my medical bills
were paid all these years. My weeks have been punctuated by

at least three visits from the doctor or the dentist and I've gotten
half my pay. Afraid Timex might take my $8 a week away, I
don't mention being labeled *A Guinea Pig for the Atomic Age*

by scientists at MIT and Argonne Labs in Illinois who studied
me in 1950 to set up standards for nuclear and atomic safety.
Amnesiac already, some days the tangles in my mind smooth out

and I remember 1947, open trolley car, No. 119, the last one
to bring fans to the Harvard/Yale game at the Bowl. A caravan
of cars crawled up Chapel Street, bumper to bumper. Football

fans held on to trolley straps like flies. One of them gave me
a seat. My son held my arm, put pennies in my hand for me to
throw to kids waiting on the streets. At Oak Street Cemetery,

the trolley leaned as if into a grave—my son told me it was
from weight of three sailors on leave, white hats cocked,
their arms around two women in seamed stockings.

I am 79. Will it ever be my turn to ring the trolley bell?

Codifier

Rikki Santer

You strained
to hear
the teacup

clatter, the pink
chatter while
spectral dust

glistened
in your
ears.

Valedictorian
tethered to
itemizing

the heat and
cold of stellar
fingerprints,

census taker
of the flaring
up, caving in,

and going out.
*Star light, star
bright* by candle

light atop
your childhood
roof you basked

in the sort of
and *as if,*
counting

constellations
thatched on
their velvet grid

of indifference.
Then Wellesley
Radcliffe, Harvard

to nurse your
spectrographs,
your dense flocks

of stars—400,000,
a lifetime's
tally. Orion

deep and wide,
spiral arms
of galaxies,

supernova
remnants—
you relished

their rewind
of time.
Your life's

orbit not as
effervescent
as it could be

but still
you perched,
devotee

on tiptoes
to launch
from your

threshold
to become
a fine girl kissed

over and over
by the quenched
lips of history.

Annie Jump Cannon (1863-1941) was an American astronomer whose cataloging work was instrumental in the development of contemporary stellar classification.

In the French Laundry

Renny Christopher

My grandmother never knew what was French about it,
only that their specialty was fancy, difficult work
on the clothes of the wealthy. She ironed collars and cuffs
on the shirts of men who could well afford her labor.
She wasn't good at math, so I'm sure she never figured
as she ironed, her hair tied in a torn bandana to keep her sweat
from dripping on the linen, how much she earned
for each collar, each cuff—this many shirts for a dollar,
this many dollars for the rent. But I am good at math.
I know that each dozen shirts cost her two thousand
heartbeats, three hundred thirty drops of sweat.

My grandmother was a semi-literate working-class woman who held jobs in laundries and in a small factory that produced hydraulic motors for bomb bay doors in WWII aircraft, among other places.

Seamstress

Memye Curtis Tucker

Margaret, lady of alterations,
have mercy on me
on the arm that cannot stretch
as far as its sister, on the shoulder
that rises each morning in excitement—
Margaret, Margaret—

make me perfect. Take my collars
flapping, the buttonholes
already raveling when I bring them home,
the plackets made by the blind, the broken stitches—
all these injured ones—take them,
Margaret, heal them.

I will return on Thursday, though it rain,
though ice freeze in your doorway
I will pour out my purse
and stand before your three-way mirror.
I will take home
all that you have mended.

*Margaret Carman was a caring seamstress who for many years had a shop in
Marietta, Georgia. I am told that when she died a few years ago, this poem was
read at her funeral. It has also been set as an art song for piano and soprano
by composer Beth Wiemann (on CD:* Why Performers Wear Black, *Albany
Records (NY and UK) Troy 675).*

Ella, in a square apron, along Highway 80

Judy Grahn

She's a copper-headed waitress,
tired and sharp-worded, she hides
her bad brown tooth behind a wicked
smile, and flicks her ass
out of habit, to fend off the pass
that passes for affection.
She keeps her mind the way men
keep a knife—keen to strip the game
down to her size. She has a thin spine,
swallows her eggs cold, and tells lies.
She slaps a wet rag at the truck drivers
if they should complain. She understands
the necessity for pain, turns away
the smaller tips, out of pride, and
keeps a flask under the counter. Once,
she shot a lover who misused her child.
Before she got out of jail, the courts had pounced
and given the child away. Like some isolated lake,
her flat blue eyes take care of their own stark
bottoms. Her hands are nervous, curled, ready
to scrape.
The common woman is as common
as a rattlesnake.

For the Cashier at T.R. Wolfe's Toy and Candy

Lisa Dordal

To enter the pinched interior
of T.R. Wolfe's Toy and Candy,

was to risk your squint
that branded every kid

a thieving urchin.
Your hair pulled back

into a coarse, gray stone,
your face bony and sad—

as we'd tap our fingers
against the counter glass

to pronounce our choice
of pink cigarettes cloaked

in sugary smoke. Or,
from the sundry collection

of jigsaw puzzles, lining
the store's high-shelved

perimeter: our choice
of Barbie and Ken's

dream house, the cockpit
of a Concorde, UFO's

over a Midwest wheat farm.
Puzzles that would spread

like sea garbage
across our bedroom floors.

How can it be that this
is what was given you?

Not a pursuit of quiet,
brainy labor: reading the ash

in Nile River mud.
Or probing the loss

of an ancient grave—
head to head, a girl and a boy,

and beads too many
to count. Only this,

the daily repetition
of warm coins passing

from our hands into yours.
And how can I not

admire you for your refusal
to feign contentment.

Whatever it was you wanted,
getting us instead.

Unknown Woman Miner

Sheila Packa

Cold shop. Bleak light.
She turns to face the layoff.
The company, she's never trusted.
The whistle blew. Inside, hard
to tell day from night.
Safety glasses, standard issue.
Her hair combed from bobby pins
into corkscrew curls.
Fluorescent buzz.
Denim overalls. Kerchief.
Her pants have a hole through.
She blows black soot from her nose.
She wears a wool plaid sweater.
Her jacket's slung on the chair.
In the back, a front end loader signals.
Her hand rests on the table. Nobody
doubts the fact she's able. It's rough.
She does what she does.
She will drive home
at morning to girls who look after
themselves. They fight.
It's hard to sleep. Her joints ache
her lunch pail's rusted.
And in the back pocket of her pants
something to protect herself.

At the Factory Where My Mother Worked

Maria Mazziotti Gillan

Once when I was seventeen, I visited the factory
where my mother worked. It was on the second floor
up a flight of narrow, rickety stairs, and when I opened
the door, the noise of sewing machines slapped my face.

I searched for my mother in the close-packed row
of women bent over their sewing. The floor manager
picked up one of the pieces my mother had finished,
screamed, "You call this sewing?" and threw the coat

on the floor. The tables were lit by bare light bulbs,
dangling down on cords. I had never seen the place
where my mother worked. She thought we should be
protected from all that was ugly and mean

in the grown-up world. "Children should be children,"
she'd say. "They'll learn trouble soon enough.
We don't need to tell them about it." She did not answer
the floor walker. Instead she bent her head over her sewing,

but not before I saw the shame in her face.

My Mother Comes Home Crying from GE

Ann Clark

My father, who works swing shift
and makes Campbell's Tomato Soup
and grilled cheese for me every day
when I get home from kindergarten,
asks what's wrong hon, what's wrong,
why are you back early, are you sick,
but she is still going oh, oh, oh, out
loud like me or my brother when we cry,
as if she has skinned her knees,
and I sit at the white and silver
kitchen table and swing my legs
and wait for soup, and she says
he took my idea, he took it and said
it was his after he promised to present
it to engineering, he didn't give me credit;
they gave him a thousand shares
in the company and when I told him
he stole my idea, he just smiled
and said sure I did, how are you
going to prove it you little, oh, oh,
and her knees are hurt again so
she can't say the words, and smoke
is choking the kitchen because
my grilled cheese is burned
so I know my soup will have
 a thick, dark skin like a scab.

For the Women Who Ride Buses

Nancy Kerrigan

Rosa, since 1955 you've sat, and sat, and sat
in our minds on that Montgomery city bus

would not give up your seat to a white man.
You weren't the first black woman who refused

to go to the back of the bus, but you are the one
etched in the black and white of our memory.

You sat there dignified in your cloth coat
with your hat on, staring out of that bus window.

Were you planning dinner under that hat,
plotting to change history, or just plain tired?

How many bus rides did it take to make you seethe,
steam rising up through your straw pill box,

before you decided not to move? Your own name
not among the P's in my 1980 encyclopedia.

In that decade of *Father Knows Best*, my mother worked
outside the home too, wearing a hat much like yours.

Often she neglected to take it off while she cooked dinner.
Mornings, she ran in high heels to catch her two buses,

consumed one library book after the next, the commute so long.
Some days rain washed away her makeup, or was it rain?

Thanks to the women who traveled unfamiliar routes before me,
I drive to my own office where I listen to the plight of women

not behind the wheels of their lives, waiting in the rain
for buses to take them to the night shift at Walmart.

Back at the Office

Grey Held

In the designated smoking area
behind vending machines,
it's just Iveta, me, and Basra
from Somalia, the new employee
with a scar from a machete
on her lovely throat. *Summa*
cum laude from Oxford, she's working
the Global Economy on an American
green card, telemarketing
in the cubicle down the hall.
Iveta has worked the mail room
for thirteen years: sorting, metering,
packaging, measuring her waning
Slavic accent by the yardstick
of democracy. Lighting up a Parliament,
she tells me of her collection of coins
from Yugoslavia. She takes from her pocket,
a shiny 1931 ten *dinara*, places it
double-headed eagle side up
in my palm. The metal is old
as the country she was minted in,
the country that no longer exists.

My First Pink Slip

Mary Langer Thompson

Not a lacy half or whole
silk of lingerie, but
a sheer missive
delivered today, needing
my unfashionable signature
saying I received it, not
that I agree not to cling
to a position gone.

The smooth Board decided
in private session,
secret even to Victoria,
taking action pursuant
to code section 44951
to unclasp me.

Four a.m. I awake
under a rusty moon
in a cold-hot sweat,
neglected in my negligee
drenched in worry.
I've finally been noticed.

Hedda Sterne

Tim Vincent

Her colors produce a unique frisson
And the force lines streak through like rays of light
Her brushes soaking in old coffee cans
Cigarettes floating in melted ice cubes
From a crowded viewing the other night
She's too old for this studio show rut
But it's the kind of life one can't give up
To do what, teach in the local high school?
Work as a docent in the museum?
deKooning once kept alive on ketchup
It's a certain kind of hard-won freedom
And the form it takes is secondary
What matters is healing the wounds of youth
And finding joy in an indifferent world.

Hedda Sterne was the only female member of the Irascibles, the 1950's New York group of abstract expressionists that included Rothko, deKooning, and others.

Something Important

Edwin Romond

for Maureen Kosa

"Then, something important has been done ..."   —Robert Bly

Search all you want but
you'll never find her name
in *People Magazine* or
The National Enquirer where
pages are littered with Lindsay Lohan,
and the Kardashians. You won't
see her doing the cha-cha on *Dancing
with the Stars*, she's too much of a master
teacher to ever be *The Apprentice*, and
you'll never catch her in a screaming, hair-
pulling fist fight on *Jerry Springer*.
There's been no camera crew
filming her those thousands of mornings
doing the crucial work of teaching
kids to read, teaching kids to speak,
and teaching kids to write.
Ryan Secrest was nowhere to be found
all those prime time evenings when
she graded papers till her eyes ached
and all those Saturdays and Sundays
doing the heroic, unseen work
of preparing lessons for her classes.
In a world that seems to honor idiots
instead of excellence this poem praises
a woman who spent decades
of autumns and winters and springs
doing something important that
never made the front page but
is engraved deeply and forever
into the hearts of the students she loved.

I Award My Own Nobel Prize to Rosalind Franklin

Allison Thorpe

By choice she did not emphasize her feminine qualities ... There was never lipstick to contrast with her straight black hair, while at the age of thirty-one her dresses showed all the imagination of English blue-stocking adolescents. So it was quite easy to imagine her the product of an unsatisfied mother who unduly stressed the desirability of professional careers that could save bright girls from marriages to dull men ... Clearly Rosy had to go or be put in her place. The former was obviously preferable because, given her belligerent moods, it would be very difficult for Maurice [Wilkins] to maintain a dominant position that would allow him to think unhindered about DNA ... The thought could not be avoided that the best home for a feminist was in another person's lab.

—James Watson (about Rosalind Franklin) from his book *The Double Helix*

Here, Honey, take it.
You earned the damn thing.
You were just too serious for them,
head down to work,
science firm in your eyes.

Enough with the schooled history
that didn't include your contribution,
Watson's admission of stealing
glances at your work, using your
ideas to rush his DNA discovery.

They planted you in a corner,
enjoyed keeping you in shadows,
whispered you the "dark lady,"
offered no admission
to that entitled club of men.

Better to have popped a button or two?
Juggled test tubes for a laugh?

Baked cookies?
Anything to apologize
for the curves
under the lab coat?

But that was not your way.
So this award is for choosing
profession over lipstick,
diligence before the dress,
the strength to rise above
your place in the world.

Rosalind Franklin was a fascinating woman whose scientific accomplishments were overlooked for a long time.

Unknown to the World,
the World to Someone

Number 99

kerry rawlinson

Ninety-nine arm-hairs rising on end
with my lover's first red-beard-prickled
                    kiss;

ninety-nine spasms in time when two
hearts beat synchronously and a fractured
                    world

becomes one. Ninety-nine feathers
plucked like a fistful of quivering
                    quail,

my delicate skeleton sucked white
in a heady new sun. And now,
                    tracing

the family tree, it leads her back
to me: a Number in a registry.
                    Squaw.

i am raven's caw; i am frog spawn; i am
necklace of bear-claw; i am quill-vest; i am
                    snow-white

rabbit paw. i am canoe filled with man-spore,
portaged to a white-tent's census-page:
                    nameless.

Ninety-nine months of blind winter
blizzards, with only my loon-soul cry to
                    pierce

the grieving emptiness of sky; ninety-
nine moose-skins cleaned to keep us
                    dry.

Ninety-nine glistening dragonfly wings
flickering in dreams of home, and early
        Spring.

Ninety-nine plump summer squirrels
trapped; ninety-nine mosquitoes
        slapped.

Ninety-nine contractions suffered—
subtracted from a nation of numbered
        placentas—

to birth my sweet daughter, *Kicâpân*.
Ninety-nine moon-tides of blood did i offer
        the flood

of your flushed generation, streams from my
denigrated lands; memory on how you must
        swim.

Ninety-nine owls guard my offspring's
skin, tingling with ninety-nine strands of
        birdsong

that i thread through your veins, braided
with sweetgrass, sage, and lonely
        waterfalls.

The ninety-nine stars that flash in your
hands, are the ninety-nine stones that cradle
        my grave.

*During colonial domination, many indigenous peoples around the world were
belittled, if not directly persecuted; their customs and ways of life largely
eradicated. North America was no exception. Although the woman being
addressed in this poem assumes that Number 99 (her Great-Great-
Grandmother) was Manitoba Cree, she has no evidence of her existence other
than this number; and family lore.*

Crazy Quilt

Lenore Hart

I can imagine all five sisters gathered around the table
        working with needle and thread to patch together the pieces
        of outgrown lives: drop-waist blue sailor dresses,
        white flannel gowns, lush red velvet scraps from a party dress,
        moth-eaten gray wool of a dead mother's coat.
        But none of it fits neatly, the odd shapes all sizes, colors, textures.

They turn them this way and that. Squinting, murmuring.
        In the end all they can make of the past is a crazy quilt,
        a wild collage refusing any set pattern, any known design.
        It might hold if they embroider stubborn edges, force seams
        that don't quite meet, suture holes and gaps with fiddleheads
        stitched of pale Chinese silk, the fronds fierce-toothed tigers' jaws.
        Nearby dark green ivy twines to border the soft black velvet
        next to a square of gray serge ripped from a nameless man's suit.

This dull stain could almost pass for a brown-petaled flower.
        My Aunt Maude's finger or perhaps Viola's, needle-pricked,
        shed a portent that couldn't be dabbed away. No amount
        of cleaning ever removes this blot where old blood mars cloth.
        The same that later fatally soaked the sheets of a childbirth bed.
        These two shared the same fate and left few other marks on life:
        three creased sepia photos, two gravestones, one motherless child.

Here a red flower with yellow stamens grows on a verdant ground
        of dark dotted silk. My grandmother Elfair surely placed it there.
        Only an artist's eye would choose that bright fan of color.
        Finished, like her paintings, after she laid aside oils and brushes
        forever and turned to diapers, skinned knees, and an early death.

On the hem curved blue thread spins up into a bouquet of fantastic knots,
        then stops suddenly as a flawed heart. No doubt sewn by Grace,
        who at sixteen thought a traveling man with soft hands
        would love and marry her. Left alone to explain a growing belly
        she filled her pockets with broken bricks and walked into the lake
        behind our house. Perhaps the cold comfort
        of tannin-brown water warmer, kinder than the fate
        reserved for curious girls back then.

These sure lines tracked like railroad crossings tie all the squares
        together. Plain, steady, enduring along, the ones laid in
        by my great aunt, Theodosia. The last and youngest sister,
        she survived it all: bad blood, worse men, stillborn babies,
        cancer, a drunkard husband, an elderly invalid father. The only one
        of five to greet old age and scoff at it. To end her days believing
        the dead returned each night, climbing in the windows
        of her tiny Florida bungalow to clean and sweep the floors.
        She died childless, holding onto my father's hand,
        her dead sister's youngest son.

Now the quilt is mine. I can repair torn edges and gnawed moth-holes.
        But I cannot piece together five lost lives. The faces of my aunts
        and my grandmother in the old photos are secretive and still.
        Under black Irish brows ten grave green eyes stare back,
        not acknowledging my gaze, not rejecting it.
        The little I know of them would not fill one spotless page.
        Still, their quilt survives.
        It warns me to make my own life whole,
        out of patches and shreds,
        lest it remain a puzzling fragment like this
        unfinished work on my wall:
        silent cloth, loud pattern, busy canvas of movement, frozen.
        Never completed, never mended into anything truly whole.

Display of Kitchen Utensils

Maxine Susman

(Shelburne Museum, Burlington VT)

On this wall, along these shelves
hundreds of kitchen tools gathered
to rest, every kind to make work light,
make more, make do through days
of weeks of seasons in cycle—
food, clothing, candles, tonics—
no home could claim to own so many
but every housewife knew her share,
the tool best suited to her purpose

to turn, lift, sift, pour, ladle, cradle,
peel, pit, stew, boil, bake, shape, skim,
stir, skewer, trim, dye, weave, darn, knit,
scour, scrub, drain, hang, shake, strain,
stir, spread, dry, stuff, scrape, wipe, fill.
Tools taken down, used, then put away
against the next time when she'd reach
for one to fit her task, fill an hour
to the brim, dough rising in the pans.

Cemetery

Eileen Moeller

Women not changed, but glorified

Faithful unto death.
Archangel, sister,
mother cradling
two stillborn babes,
veiled figure
leaning on a cross,
siren draped over an anchor,
armless muse setting
the soul free from its coffin.

Yarrow, Wunder, Benson, Moore, Pepper

Wife of, wife of,
daughter of, daughter of,
men keen as Lincoln,
sacred as temples;
men who were lions,
pillars broken by time;
men complex as Celtic crosses,
big as spired cathedrals.
Men sure to rise up again when
the trumpet of judgment cries.

Childs, Claghorn, Hex. McNutt, Lippincott

Emmas, Helenas, Annas, Mildreds,
Maudes, Marthas, Josephines,
put here, by husbands and fathers,
their lives ephemeral and little understood,
their effigies, soot dark, or eaten away
by the city's acrid air, slipping them
further down the ladder into mystery.
Their names, wreathed in cut stone ivy,
lily of the valley, shiny marble oak leaves,

their bodies surrendered, personhood
indecipherable as rain smoothed words,
beds of tangled crabgrass, thistleweed,
ribwort, dandelion, laced with cricket song.

DayStar

Rita Dove

She wanted a little room for thinking
but she saw diapers steaming on the line,
a doll slumped behind the door.

So she lugged a chair behind the garage
to sit out the children's naps.

Sometimes there were things to watch—
the pinched armor of a vanished cricket,
a floating maple leaf. Other days
she stared until she was assured
when she closed her eyes
she'd only see her own vivid blood.

She had an hour, at best, before Liza appeared
pouting from the top of the stairs.
And just what was mother doing
out back with the field mice? Why,

building a palace. Later
that night when Thomas rolled over and
lurched into her, she would open her eyes
and think of the place that was hers
for an hour—where
she was nothing,
pure nothing, in the middle of the day.

Sunday Greens

Rita Dove

She wants to hear
wine pouring.
She wants to taste
change. She wants
pride to roar through
the kitchen till it shines
like straw, she wants

lean to replace
tradition. Ham knocks
in the pot, nothing
but bones, each
with its bracelet
of flesh.

The house stinks
like a zoo in summer,
while upstairs
her man sleeps on.
Robe slung over
her arm and
the cradled hymnal,

she pauses, remembers
her mother in a slip
lost in blues,
and those collards,
wild-eared,
singing.

The Woman in the House

Bridget Grieve-Carslon

At night, as a teenager,
I'd watch Fred and Ginger,
the dance team on the television.
This was in the days when Fred was considered the expert,
long before it ever occurred to anyone,
Even while we were watching,
Ginger was doing it all
backwards,
in heels.

One night my mother walked through the hallway
from the kitchen
to find me lying on the living room sofa,
subdued by the August heat.
There is so little time
between finishing the dishes and deciding to talk to me
that when she comes up and stands in front of me,
blocking the television
with her plump pregnant belly,
water drops still hang from her usually ragged fingernails,
giving them the appearance of long perfect nails.

It isn't until years later that
I remember what she said to me that night.
You know love isn't really like that,
she said, as she turned to Fred and Ginger.
But I wasn't listening.
I loved anything perfect back then.
I loved the first few days after my mother got her hair done
and nothing she did would mess it.
And when she would dress for a party in a new, clean floral dress
and put on makeup,
and gone
were the runs in her nylons,
stains on her clothes,
and dark circles under her eyes.
I wasn't listening that night.

I was marveling at her perfect fingernails
and the way the droplets of water that hung from them
glistened by the light of the television.
She was just my mother back then.
The woman in the house
who did everything,
while pregnant,
with kids in diapers.

This poem is about an actual conversation I had with my mother when I was a young teenage girl. What she said to me had an effect on me as I grew up and became an adult and a mother myself.

Aunt Vilma

Paul Martin

Thin and hollow cheeked when she didn't
have her teeth in, she'd fire up
a Lucky Strike and wave away concern

as "shit for the birds"
and I could almost imagine the girl
stealing from her parents' boarders, running

away in the night, dancing on bars,
a brief marriage, abortion or a given up infant,
my older brother recalling with wide eyes

the time she flashed a tit at him.
"Oh, she was a firecracker, your aunt,"
offered old Mr. George deep in his cups

at the Hunky Club, as though that explained the girl
who wanted more than that smoky factory town,
even if she didn't know what it was

that night she spent sick and alone
in a bar until Leonard passed through
on his way to work and gave the owner money

for a room and a doctor, saying he'd pay
whatever it cost when he returned,
the two of them settling into a quiet life,

stopping by with her at the wheel
of the '54 DeSoto with its huge tail fins
to sit again at the kitchen table,

showing us how to blow smoke rings,
slipping between funny faces
and a sudden, faraway silence.

How She Lived

Cinthia Ritchie

Crazy,
we swore,
the things she did
and said and all the times
she called complaining
the feds or was the CIA
were after her.
Why should we care,
she was far away,
a nervous voice on the phone,
and when guilt soured our stomachs,
we mailed her money:
there, we consoled ourselves,
I did something, now
I can go on with my life
and forget about her.

But we couldn't,
that was the thing, the way her words
hung in our minds, weighing down every
act until no matter what we did: picking out fruit
in the supermarket or combing our hair for work,
the shadow of her words weighed the spaces
behind us. When she died, we were relieved.
And angry. We were stunned and torn and flayed.
We had known, we reassured each other.
We had been expecting it for years.

A lie:
we thought she would always be there,
an omniscient narrator, a soliloquy of our
past, the way she wouldn't let us forget
the things that had happened, or maybe
it was some type of displaced goodness,
the way she forced us to remember,
not by talking nor silence,
but the stubborn fact of her craziness.

They were trying to kill her, she said,
they implanted microchips in her head,
stuck things up her ass and down her throat
until she couldn't sleep couldn't eat
couldn't do anything and could we
please please please send money
so she could buy food or clothes or
something for the dog? Blood on our hands,
all of us, like Lady Macbeth, except we didn't
do the actual killing, we were too refined,
too proper. We kept ourselves insulated
inside our neat little lives. No mess,
no pain, and hey, don't tell me
'cause I don't want to know.

But this is what we can't forget,
what torments us, what we can't bear
to talk about. When they went back
to her apartment, there was nothing there
but a mattress, cracked dishes, old clothing
scattered about the floor. Living like that for
years, and we didn't know, how could we
have known, yet this is still our fault, what
we must live with, the guilt we all must bear:
that we never asked. That none of us ever said,
describe your house, tell me where you live.
Tell me, tell us about your life.

"How She Lived" is about my sister, who died of eating disorder related complications fifteen years ago. She had become increasingly distraught and paranoid in the last few years of her life and I regret that I didn't do more to try and save her. Instead, I wrote a poem. A small thing perhaps, but not enough.

Power and Light

Paula Sergi

When she's out of money again, flat broke despite
her frugal coupon clipping, she shoves the unpaid power
and light bill to the back of her mother's hand-carved
maple desk, closes the drawer,
and starts a project from whatever can be found.
She's good at drawer closings, discounting
what can't be figured on paper. The day her husband died
at the lake leaving three small kids and one on the way,
she stood in the unfinished kitchen, made a meal
from canned tuna, then shined our best shoes
for morning. One week later she found a dachshund pup,
and began her private crying. I have heard her
ripping sheets for café curtains, seen her running
stitch turn a scarf into a valence. She'd paint mismatched
spindle back chairs with colors from the hall
and upstairs bath—turquoise, rose, even avocado.
She'd toss a quilt made from outgrown skirts
over the faded couch and lie there,
holding the ache, rocking it to sleep. I've seen her
make soup from an old beef bone,
some celery, whatever else she could find.
She's repotted leafless plants, just to imagine
how callused stems might bloom.

Remembrance

Psyche North Torok

In memory of Rose Molnar Török, 10/20/1888 – 7/17/1932

Maybe there is nothing left to say,
with just a headstone and
a rose to mark your grave.

But let's talk about seasickness,
morning sickness:
you sucked the ship's icicles to
ease the nausea.

Let's talk about endurance,
about odds,

your thirteen children—
the one stillborn—
how you labored,
in so many ways.

And let's mention your
husband, dashing
bowls of soup against the wall,
and all the days you went hungry.

Maybe there is nothing left to recall
but the buckets and scrub rags,
the iron pot, meager broth.

Oh, but let's remember your hunger,
sharp as a gnawed bone,

sharp as a needle,
shattered dishes,
your butcher knife.

Maybe there is nothing more to ask
but how to transmute hunger.

Feed me, Grandmother. Find a way.
Let nourishment be your will for me, your legacy.
Bequeath your heirloom strength.
Give me this answer, this memory,
the secret you took with you
on your last, most memorable voyage.

Some of What I Know About Her

Charlene Langfur

I am not as small as she was nor as strong,
you can see if you look at the picture,
the hint of a smile even as she works,
the dreamy glow about her,
living in air, birthing babies, getting on,
planting corn season after season, the giant green stalks
between the meadows and the river,
the Hackensack River ran through the area then.
I was born in the hospital in the city
of Hackensack years later,
but for me always she was on the farm
planting and making pillows with chicken feathers,
watching wrestling on TV when the TV finally came,
she was aghast at it and loved it at the same time.
She worked until she was tired
and slept until she had to wake, she raised chickens and pigs,
said goodbye to Prague and the Charles River years before,
pushed off right across Europe to America
where there were seven Czech farms,
Little Ferry, New Jersey, USA,
this was the way, she followed the others,
joined the *Sokol Hall*, sent her children
to pick strawberries and blackberries for 5 cents an hour,
sent my Uncle Joe to WWI,
he was gassed in the trenches and never the same after it,
drinking hard liquor at the bar on Indian Lake to forget,
she loved all of it, planted beans, tomato, marigold,
it never got old, of course my father forgot
none of it, he was the youngest, told me how the meadows
were filled with garbage, the reeds blowing in the wind
like angels on a summer night paved over,
companies moving there from all over the world
but all he could think of was the farm, the mornings
when the sun rose over the city, the Hudson so close,
and then the meadows with outlets to come, a football stadium,
soon, Good Lord yes, the Super Bowl,

there where the birds in the meadows rested on the tall reeds,
a place so wild and wily, with eddies under the black water
in the deep pools. She knew what to do.
I know, she lived strong, well, keen,
Mary Havel worked, lived as a former,
on the rich black soil of Northern New Jersey
in the greenest of meadows.

Shadows Behind *The Daughters of Edward Darley Boit*

Sheila A. Murphy

The Daughters of Edward Darley Boit, John Singer Sargent (1882)
Museum of Fine Arts, Boston

I

Only a child of privilege could lean
in studied languor, at fourteen,
against a vase, one of a pair,
that flanked a foyer's darkened air.
The sheen of glaze, a bird in flight,
mirror the gleam of girls in white,
wearing pinafores starched, uncreased.
The youngest, Julia, sits, at ease,
with a doll between her legs, just so.
I gaze at Julia, long and slow—
her ruffled wrists and turned-in toes.
Even her doll wears frilly clothes.

II

Another Julia comes to light
who would have hovered out of sight
ironing those pretty pinafores.
My grandmother Julia, widowed
at forty, had a brood of five to raise.
I walk on braided rugs she made.
Her Julia, my mother, in 1916,
graduated high school, the immigrants' dream.
She learned shorthand and leaned on prayer,
quoted Longfellow, Donne, and Shakespeare.
One Julia in oils, and two on my mind,
in Sargent's shadows intertwined.

*My grandmother Julia O'Sullivan Lehan, eldest of 12, emigrated from
Kenmare, Ireland, to Boston, at age 17. She worked as a domestic before
marriage and after her husband died of influenza when she was pregnant with
their fifth child. My mother, Julia Lehan Gallagher, was first in her family to
graduate high school.*

Grandmother of the Fields

Lillo Way

Come on out, Josephine, come out
of your log cottage at the edge of the long-needled pines
that drape the roof, turning the shingles green,
the trees themselves tinted blue in the light
of the Ed Sullivan Show.

    You, watching the mahogany console,
    put down your long-necked Schlitz,
    rise from your patchouli-warmed, cigarette-cozied spot
    under the dark cracked beams, and take me

up the narrow stairs to a bed nook where you
have sprinkled violet toilet water on pillow feathers
so I might sleep to the sound of semitrailers
straining gears on the hill road. I'm asking you,

    Josephine of hollyhocks and marigolds,
    set down the fishing pole and give me
    the strong brown hand that in the morning
    trembled nervous to braid a young girl's hair.

Come, Josephine, stretch yourself on the davenport
exhausted, and read me chapters in Old Yeller
while the spaniel named for Tom Sawyer
naps on the braided oval rug. Come here,

    dress me as a bride in your window curtains
    and pose me in the chestnut-secreting sedge
    where I, solemn, grip my marigold bouquet
    as you kneel behind your Brownie camera.

And quick now climb down the tractor
to clomp your boots through rufous fields,
your wooded creeks and cowlicks,
before they are transformed

into rows of small, identical, white houses—
almost at the very second your lids
last lower over those blind
green Josephine eyes.

In This Photograph Taken in Arizona

Pat Hale

My father's mother holds a rattlesnake,
caught and killed not three feet from their back door,
out by the clothesline where she hangs the sheets.
She holds its flat head level with her shoulders;
its tail reaches to her skirt hem. She's smiling,
her head tilted as if puzzling out
the illogical twists of a child's retelling
of a story. She pinches the snake
between her thumb and forefinger.
It's a cigarette someone's dared her to smoke.
Traces of her penciled writing on the back
show through, turning the desert landscape
into a field of snow crossed by sparrows.
"This is the last of the snakes," she writes.
But how does she know what else lives
under the floor boards, what else
might cross the snow while they are sleeping?
Caroline once found a snake coiled up
in a pot under the sink. She slammed
the lid back on, weighted it with a cast iron pan,
went outside to think. My grandmother writes
that the snake had eight rattles. She herself
would have had eight children in eight years,
had one not been lost in the eighth month
when a can being soldered exploded,
punching her hard in the belly.
In this photo, she is framed by scrub trees
under a white sky. She casts a clear, bright shadow.

Sherpa

Paula Sergi

Someone has to haul
all our crap up hill,
make appointments, cancel,
reschedule. Make excuses. Cover
when the son's face goes red and blotchy,
nose stuffs up. Or, more alarming,
he shakes in a warm shower,
shakes under the quilt, shakes
out the words *I'll be all right*
from a sheet white face gone angular,
then *I don't know*. Someone
calls 911, ignores the neighbors'
stares, fits herself into a side seat
in the ambulance, says the word heroin
out loud, holds the puke pan, admits

she's his mother. Someone sits
with a panicked patient now pacing
in wait for the psych consult, neuro,
clergy. Someone steps to the curb
outside the hospital to hail a cab
while the son gathers his bathrobe around him,
and shuffles to the door in slippers brought
from home. Someone calls the father,
says *yes cancel everything and come*
so we can sit and weep together and alone
and hang on, as if his life depends on it.

What about the mothers of addicts? Here is a perspective on their suffering.

In a Gift Shop

Ted Kooser

Only in recent years have I begun
to notice them living among us,
and yesterday there were two more,
the one somewhere in her seventies
and in a wheelchair, and the other
younger by maybe twenty years,
helping the older woman pick out cards
from one of those squeaky revolving
racks in a shop. The older would gesture
with a weak brush of her hand to tell
the younger to turn the rack a little
and the younger would turn it, and both
would study the cards from the top
to the bottom, and once in a while
the younger would take a card down
and show it to the other, holding it
closed and then open, and the older
might nod to agree that it seemed
the right choice, or she might dismiss it
with a shake of her head with its thin
white hair, and the younger would
patiently put it back, and this went on
for what seemed a very long while
as the woman in the wheelchair slowly
assembled a little collection of cards
in her lap, and the rack turned round
as if it were the world itself (though with
a plaintive squeak), with the colorful days
passing first into the light and then out
and with hundreds of thousands of women
like these, each helping another
do something for someone not there.

Four in the Morning

Tony Howarth

too late to take   a   pill
     don't want to just lie here either
         flickers, always thought of them as solitary birds,
        said good-bye yesterday, heading south,
     pecking at the lawn eight or nine of them

               Betsy and Margaret
        they keep on at me
Mom - you've got to come and live with us
        each of them, both of them,
                   together, apart
I don't really understand how it would work

I hate all that ocean
         getting there, tracking sand
         into their houses
         worrying about a hurricane

I want to stay here, with my tall trees

     all right, here comes winter

I know, asthma, broken hip,
     that's my problem
          not yours   I'm not a cripple
        I can take   care of myself

I love going through the house and touching

         time to take his tennis trophies
        off the shelf, shine them up

I should have never

     stupid thing to do
     put the house on the market   but

I told that one family, how we rebuilt the patio
        because of termites, now they're chewing
        the porch

        sabotaged the other family too, told them
        how the basement floods every time it rains
I could take down the sign

        they'd raise such a fuss
          Mom, you promised

I want to tell everybody straight out, no

           this   house   is   who   I   am

I want to stay right here, I'm not alone

                  the way you think I am

I have to tell that young couple   tomorrow

    tell them

        the price of the house just went up
        thousands   not going to   budge
        that's the new price   or
I could maybe

        I wish

               will it ever be daylight

Meantime

Karen Torop

she says again, pauses, savoring her story,
eyes lively, still May blue. She delights in the surprising
simultaneity of happenings, *meantime* hovering over

her words, waiting to connect this with that. Meantime,
her fingers fret with the napkin, her brows ruffle and meet as she
strains to hear her daughters' words, what they are laughing about.

What she's missed she means to know. Meantime, bits
of food cling to her lips – how unlike her
to be stooped when she stands, bent as she walks. A lapse

in memory, the irritated search for a name, and the stale breath of age –
meantime, a muffled panic about falls, illness, winter,
her heartbeat in tumult at times, a din in her ears. Her hand clutches

the railing and time means everything now, the umbrella arching over,
pressing her down: smaller and smaller she grows,
bones loosely covered, mean as spokes.

110th Birthday

Ted Kooser

Helen Stetter

Born into an age of horse-drawn wagons
that knocked and rocked over rutted mud
in the hot wake of straw, manure and flies,
today she glides to her birthday party
in a chair with sparkling carriage wheels,
along a lane of smooth gray carpeting
that doesn't jar one petal of the pink corsage
pinned to her breast. Her hair is white
and light as milkweed down, and her chin
thrusts forward into the steady breezes
out of the next year, and the next and next.
Her eyelids, thin as old lace curtains,
are drawn over dreams, and her fingers
move only a little, touching what happens
next, no more than a breath away. Her feet,
in fuchsia bedroom slippers, ride inches above
the world's hard surface, up where she belongs,
safe from the news, and now and then, as if
with secret pleasure, she bunches her toes
the way a girl would, barefoot in sand
along the Niobrara, just a century ago.

Abandoned Wife with Two Sons

Elayne Clift

In the supermarket,
She'd look like any other
wife and mother.
You'd never even notice
her red hair and glasses,
if she were only sniffing melons,
or scratching fresh tomatoes
off her list.

But at the intersection,
She catches your eye.
Her sign says "Please Help.
Abandoned wife, two sons."
Their school photos
are taped to her placard
and you think, how handsome.
She must have been young
when she had them.

You rummage in your purse,
And for once,
Long for the red light
to last. For a moment,
you consider pulling over.
"What happened?" you want to ask.
"Would you like to come to dinner?"

Instead, you roll the window down,
Motioning with your finger,
And what you hope is a friendly smile.
You drop a dollar in her cup.
"Thank you! God Bless," she says.
And then, For one eternal second,
Your eyes meet. And there you are.
Two women. Two mothers.
One who will drive home,
And one who will not.

Blue Violin

Sherry Rind

In the twilight between a slice of streetlight
and the 7-Eleven window's slushies and cereals,
a fat woman in a muumuu
tucks into a popsicle-blue violin.

Bleached like last year's birdnest
her hair tips south
in the wind of comings and goings.
The notes she flings across the parking lot
scatter like sparrows fleeing shoppers' feet.

She shakes the bow over the open case.
Pay!
Pay for the wallop
time has given her, a left hook
staggering her against the wall.

In the far lane
I lean out my car window to hear
her scolding three smoke-blowing shoppers
for being too young
to hear what she has to say.

Women's Prison

Joseph Bathanti

Two Sundays a month, darkness still abroad,
we round up the kids and bundle them
into a restored salvaged Bluebird school bus,
repainted green, and make the long haul

to Raleigh where their mothers are locked
in Women's Prison. We pin the children's names
and numbers to their coats, count them
like convicts at lights-out. Sucking thumbs,

clutching favorite oddments to cuddle as they ride
curled in twos on patched sprung benches,
they sleepwalk bashfully, the little aged,
into the belly of the bus, eyes nailed to its floor.

We feed them milk and juice, animal crackers, apples;
stop for them to use the bathroom,
and to change the ones so young, they can't help wetting.
We try singing: folk tunes and strike ballads—

as if off to picket or march with an army of babies—
but their stony faces will not yield and, finally,
their passion to disappear puts them to sleep,
not to wake until the old Bluebird jostles

through the checkpoints into the prison.
Somehow, upon reopening their eyes, they know
to smile at the twirling jagged grandeur
surrounding the massive compound: concertina—

clotted with silver scraps of dew and dawn light,
a bullet-torn shroud of excelsior, scored
in dismal fire, levitating in the savage
Sabbath sky. By then, their mothers,

in the last moments of girlish rawboned glory,
appear in baggy, sky-blue prison shifts,
their beautiful hands lifting to shield their eyes,
like saints about to be slaughtered,

as if the light is too much, the sky suddenly egg-blue,
plaintive, threatening to pale away, the sun
still invisible, yet blinding. Barefoot, weepy,
they call their babies by name and secret endearment,

touch them everywhere like one might the awakened dead.
The children remain dignified, nearly aloof
in their perfect innocence, and self-possession,
toddling dutifully into the arms of anyone

who reaches for them, even the guards, petting them too.
When visiting hours conclude, the children hand
their mothers cards and drawings, remnants
of a life they are too young to remember,

but conjure in glyphic crayon blazes.
Attempting to recollect the narrative
that will guide them back to their imagined homes,
the mothers peer from the pictures to the departing

children—back and forth, straining
to make the connection, back
and forth until the children, already fast asleep
as the bus spirits them off, disappear.

The Swimmer

Alice Pettway

Mozambique

For a moment the thin cotton
of the girls' dresses floating
around their slim bodies
made me think below me
was only a wave of jelly fish.
And then their six heads
freshly braided were a sandbar
festooned with seaweed.
Then a shoe fell,
descending more quickly
than the hands and arms
and faces beneath me, and then
they were six dead girls
sinking under me
because no one
had taught them to swim
like I could
from our capsized boat.

My feet circled beneath me,
restless fish, and I counted
as each girl came to rest
on the bottom,
engulfed in a sparkle of sand.
I stretched my toes down to them,
my head bobbing, a buoy
above the moving ocean.
Green salt kissed me
like a lover might have kissed
the drowned girls in a few years.
A fisherman came
and lifted me away from my sisters
in arms that smelled of crab and sweat.
The nets I rested on
as we drifted home were the color
of pink nail polish underwater.

Who I Was

Paul Martin

One late afternoon after high school
basketball practice,
walking through the quiet halls,
I saw them, three old women in babushkas,
dark stocking and sneakers,
emptying waste baskets, mopping, polishing
the classrooms their grandchildren filled during the day.

The last ones from the old country,
all of them gone by now
and with them the Slovak I spoke
when I said, *Dobry den, ako sa mate?*
abruptly turning them from their work
toward me, wondering whose son I was,
their round faces slowly opening
like big, warm kitchens.

* *Dobry den, ako sa mate: Good day, how are you?*

First Indications from the Unknown Half-Sister

Maureen Tolman Flannery

> ...and then she says from somewhere out of left field
I think your father was my father too while I am thinking I don't even know
you and who the hell are you to be claiming my dad who had only two daugh-
ters and you're not one of them but then she goes on with her story of frac-
tured childhood on the cliff-rim of existence always inches from the plunge
into the canyon of hunger and her beautiful mother beaten but not beaten
down abandoned young by a brutal drunk of a husband who had dragged
them among the west's transients from bunk house to mining camp sheep
wagon to rented shack lacking every convenience barely protected from pred-
ators of the wild by my father the clandestine benefactor of their marginal
lives until I wonder how to convey my sorrow over the girlhood she does not
regret with its disastrous lessons blessings miracles since I'm flooded with
guilt about the unearned ease of my life having felt always entitled as the child
of the landed because the rancher was my father so that I could anticipate
everything easy just because I had been born to the woman he married and
not the one he must have loved and by what specious privilege did I expect to
be ranch-housed and helped with homework comforted always with paternal
attention and a horse or a pet prairie dog if I so much as mentioned it

*Years after my ranching father had died, my sister and I were contacted by a
woman we barely knew. It seems her mother had been a cook on the ranch. She
had reason to believe that my father was her biological father. As we heard her
story and grew to know and love her, we became convinced that her suspicions
were true.*

Everything About Egypt

Edwin Romond

Music was only supposed to last
from 12:20 to one but
on St. Patrick's Day Sister Judith
seemed radiant as star dust
so on we sang
holding the geography of Egypt
for another day. I remember
our forty-two faces lighting
with Sister's love for the songs
of Ireland that afternoon. Egyptian
rivers had to wait while Vito
Carluzzi crooned, "When Irish
Eyes Are Smiling" and Stash
Jankowski belted, "Me Father's
Shillelagh." We just kept singing
and singing with the pyramids and
sphinxes growing one day older
for soon it was 1:30, then it was two
in a room filled with fifth graders
and a nun we loved, one
voice beautiful as prayer. And I,
like a lucky leprechaun, found
a pot of gold in the second row
where pretty Jane Ellen Hughes
sang "O Danny Boy" and I dreamed
in green she was really singing
"O Eddie Boy" as we walked hand
in hand along a Galway shore.
So, Sister Judith, lovely lady of God,
know that this boy in the back
remembers when we kept text books
closed to spend all afternoon in song
and that joy is an emerald river
flowing through my soul and all these years
later I need to thank you for everything
about Egypt we did not learn the day
you let the lesson plan go, one March 17th
when none of us could stop the music.

Lessons

Jennifer L. Freed

If you were that woman, sitting
every Friday in the public library, one week working
through the *who* and *how* and *why*
of simple questions whispering from your tutor's lips,
the next week learning *price* and *pay* and *sale* and *save*
and *How much does it cost?*—
if you were that woman,
then you, too,
would ask for repetition of *bag* and *back* and *bank*,
of *leave* and *leaf* and *left* and *live*,
and you would struggle to produce the English sounds
that held the meanings you still held
inside your head: the dappled murmuring of leaves
outside your childhood home, the trees
full of sweet yellow fruit you could not name in this new life,
the lives you left so you could live,
and as you moved your lips in all the unfamiliar ways
to make the sounds your tutor made, she would nod
and you would smile, but you would never
write, for you'd not yet know how
to form or read those fast, firm letters you watched pouring from her hand,
and so you'd have no way to store what you had learned
except in memory and hope,
alongside memories of why you'd never needed written words
in your native world, where your mother had taught you all the skills
of planting and harvesting and weaving and singing
that you would ever need
for living in a lush, good place,
and alongside memories
of gunfire echoing beyond the trees,
of rebels begging for or stealing food,
of soldiers from some distant city standing in your
village, barking about loyalty
and able-bodied men,
and then the memories
of jungle paths for five long nights,
of sharing food and whispered hope with others who had dared
to flee,

and the memories of the daughter and the son, both
born and grown high as your eye in the refugee camp on the border.
The English words would nestle in amidst
all this,
get lost, be found again, and you would have to try
to pull them out but leave the rest
behind, try
to let the new sounds tell you
not only the hard-edged names and places
of this brick and concrete life, but also
how to live in it—
how to take a city
bus, how to pay
for light—
and you would sit again, again, again
in a mauve chair at a round table in the library,
amidst the shelves and worlds
of words, struggling
with your *who* and *how* and *why*,
and you would not allow yourself to figure
how much it had cost,
or how much you still had to pay.
You would just smile and thank your tutor,
and come back
next Friday.

Worn Skeins

Joan Hofmann

You asked for world peace but
on your birthday you get
a saffron yellow woven silk wrap
with nubbed fibers throughout
the cloth to appease your guilt
for otherwise it may look too
precious or luxurious. As though
anyone, you included, could
stop the ache in the knobbed fingers
of the woman who hunched hours
over the cloth knotting fringe
and straightening filaments
born from the captive diligence of
mulberry silkworms to rest
neatly whorled on your shoulders
and ring your neck without
a thread other than elegance.

In the Shadows of Their Men

Programme Music

Christine Casson

Was it lightheadedness, a stomach-flutter
you felt when you read your father's letter
written from Paris, his response to your lieder?

Never mind the flurry of inspiration,
weeks when you could hardly separate pen
from paper, the years of preparation

realized in those new compositions,
and, after, your elation with everything—
the garden, conversation, your ink-stained hands.

He spoke of your forthcoming confirmation,
a Christian path chosen for his daughter
who must *devote her soul, her intelligence*

to *motherhood, home,* the highest improvements
for a young woman of your accomplishments
for whom *music must remain an ornament.*

Did you wonder, then, at your education—
a young prodigy's rigorous training,
your father's attentiveness to your playing?

You were "as gifted" as your brother,
his confidante and musical advisor
possessed of a talent surpassing his.

How quickly were you able to smother
your stricken stare, left at home to embroider?
Felix would travel to see the great Goethe,

wander Paris like a country of desire,
while you turned graciously towards marriage,
though Hensel saw what thrummed behind your eyes.

What remedy, what prospects could he propose
now that you'd slipped—diminuendo—
behind a curtain, into shadow?

Fanny Mendelssohn Hensel (1805-1847), pianist and composer, wrote at a time when it was considered unsuitable for a woman from the upper classes to have ambitions as a professional musician. Therefore, as sister to the composer Felix Mendelssohn, she was, both during her life and afterwards, overshadowed by him creatively and professionally.

Of Unforgettable

Lynn Schmeidler

I used to be Pauline Bonaparte. *Napoleon's sister does not feel fear* and youth is meant to talk on and on about itself. What I amassed: volcanoes of clothes, monsoons of jewels, folly and vanity beyond belief. I had the protection of the Pope. If six grenadiers forced me into a litter, I went where I was told.

Give me a Duchy? I'll sell it for cash. Appetites are for feeding. I threw parties and balls; I threw fits. What's the point of pretty if you can't have unreasonable? Soldiers & yellow fever sweated in my bed. Daily I bathed in fresh milk, entertained gentlemen guests from my tub. My dresses were so sheer you could see the pinks of my nipples. I needed an imperial house of propaganda to defend me. To my friends I was endlessly entertaining. To my enemies all that was wrong with the world. I made the hands of the most famous sculptor in Italy shake.

Queen of Trinkets to the last, everybody wanted me; three countries claimed me. Strange then to be invisible to wind, fists and scratches all gone. I've folded my feathers into hat boxes. I've eaten the icing off all my cakes.

Dearest Eliza

Juditha Dowd

April, 1827
Beech Grove

Dearest Eliza,

You ask after Mr. Audubon.
Last week, a letter written months ago.
Every day he tries to sell subscriptions for his book,
traveling many miles by foot and carriage.

I pray he has trimmed his dangling locks,
so in London and in Edinburgh he is received
respectfully by those who may be of help.
He is husband to his birds now,
and I am. . . I am what?

Here, I teach my students how to swim,
this body rinsed and for a moment held.

I have almost worn out the piano.

*What does it mean to sacrifice for someone else's art? My interest in Audubon
had shifted toward his remarkable wife, Lucy Bakewell, an English aristocrat
who met him soon after arriving in America. We know his observations from
published works, but few of Lucy's words survive. What was her perspective on
the arduous journey that defined their early decades together?*

Monique Braille's Confession

Susan J. Erickson

As gentle as a beguilement of butterflies,
my son's fingertips read the alphabet
of my face. I erase the punctuation
of worry from my brow. The scent
of tears disturbs Louis, so I divert
mine to water the radishes.

My habit is to kiss first
Louis' right eye—the one he punctured
playing with Simon-Rene's awl.
Then I kiss the left, blinded
by disease, as if I were Saint Lucy
and could miraculously bestow sight.

Between the pages of my Bible
I keep the holy card from Father Palluy
where Saint Lucy displays
a gold platter with two eyeballs
balanced like plump grapes
from our vineyard. Should Lucy appear
I would demand she earn her holy keep.

> (I make the Sign of the Cross
> for I do not intend sacrilege.
> Do I?)

Whatever the weather, I wear
the tight-button collar of guilt.
At every chance I read to Louis,
but always there is butter to churn,
chickens that need heads cut off.

Louis is my favorite child. Today
he leaves for the Royal Institute in Paris
where it is said they open the eyes
of the blind, lead them through
the doors of darkness.

I am not a wheel on the carriage
that takes Louis away, nor the ridged
track left in the mud. I am the patched
elbow of the republic of motherhood.

Monique Braille was the mother of Louis Braille who was accidently blinded as a young child. Louis perfected a six-dot embossed code that allowed the blind to read.

Practicing Self-Reliance

Jacqueline Doyle

> *"It is only as a man puts off from himself all external support, and stands alone, that I see him to be strong and to prevail."*
> —Ralph Waldo Emerson, "Self-Reliance" (1841)

What was she thinking,
Emerson's second wife,
when he instructed fellow Transcendentalists to
shut the door
on "importunate trifles" that
interfered with their
inspiration,
and made a list of bothersome details to beware of:
"Friend, client, child, sickness, fear, want, charity"?

She must have been just outside the door
dealing with all those trifles,
while Thoreau's mother
was busy baking pies and doughnuts for Henry, and
doing his laundry,
during his sojourn in the woods,
and Bronson Alcott's wife and children
were starving
on Transcendentalist principles,

"self-reliance" being a virtue more easily cultivated
with others to rely upon,
and no others that rely upon you,
a privilege for the manly few,

but surely a decided burden for those
virtuous Concord women,
whose names have all but disappeared from history:
Lidian, Cynthia, Abby, Anna, Louisa, Elizabeth, May,
mortals lending support to the immortals,
hardly allowed to transcend the mundane,
weighed down by trifles,

never alone, but strong, self-reliant,
prevailing.

*The women referred to include Lidian Emerson (Ralph Waldo Emerson's wife);
Cynthia Dunbar Thoreau (Henry David Thoreau's mother); Abigail (Abby)
May Alcott (Bronson Alcott's wife); Anna, Louisa, Elizabeth, and May (Abigail
and Bronson Alcott's children). See Louisa May Alcott's short story
"Transcendental Wild Oats" for a vivid picture of her mother's lot as the wife of
a Transcendentalist.*

The Dinner Table: Camille

Carmen Germain

What would she do, another winter with no heat?
How he never slept, worrying
about his paintings, other artists
starting to sell,
knowing what worked, and what didn't.
She must have begged him to think of his child.
How it would feel, pockets heavy with francs,
meat whenever they wanted.

Maybe she set it up, the still-life. Burnished
borrowed cutlery, porcelain, and glass.
Laid the tablecloth, bought fruit out of season
with whatever money they had, and hothouse lilies.
That winter he worked in coat and gloves,
she posed as serving girl, and he meant it to be
real—colors subdued, knives painted
so sharp she might slice her fingers.
The way a feast for guests should look,
drapery gracefully muted, shadows curving fruit.

Meant it, this comfort—a complement
to de Heem's *La Dessert*, the opulence of a world
where there's always enough to eat.

But then peaches flamed crimson,
blushed orange, lemons deep
in pigment, wine carafes blooming
burgundy and cobalt, white highlighting white,
cloth brushed by saffron and ivory
with a band of red. And the serving girl
bending to fuss with the flowers?
Her face luminous in blue-violet.

Splendid color, anything he felt it to be,
not what it was. All the painting
dancing in front of his eyes, all he saw.

But think of her, returning the bone-
handled knives, the plates and bowls,
butcher and baker holding out their hands,
and now the pears too ripe, bruised at the core.

Camille was an early companion of Matisse and the mother of his daughter. Provincial middle class families didn't recognize their Left Bank artist sons' mistresses but depended on these young, working-class women: sons fleeing to Paris would be taken care of until marriages were made with respectable women. The future for the unmarried, single mother could be grim.

Honored

Christine Beck

She was honored, she told herself,
honored to drop the second L
in her last name, honored to obscure
this sign of humble parentage, eager
to rise up to the level of her love,
one Dante Gabriel Rossetti.

She was honored, she knew,
lying in a bathtub, pretending
to be dead, drowned for love.
Who wouldn't want to play Ophelia?
Who wouldn't want to be painted
as the woman Hamlet loved,
who couldn't bear to live without him,
floating in the muck and mire,
roses tangled in her hair,
signifying youth, or innocence,
or some elusive longing clichéd
to death?

She was honored, even though the water
was quite chilly, cold in fact,
the promised heater on the blink,
but who was she to complain,
when the great Dante Rossetti
chose to paint her? His muse, he'd
spiffed up her name, claimed to
love her best, although two younger
models had captured his attention.

Not THE Dante, of course, this Dante
was five centuries down, but
still tangled in the myth of greatness,
still obsessed with Beatrice,
the perfection of lost love.

So, yes, she was honored, although
her fingers were bluing, although
she would spend the next five days
in bed, eventually succumb to laudanum.

But this was nothing to the honor
that awaited, the honor at her funeral,
when Rossetti put his latest poems
in her coffin, as he was riding high,
could make this sacrifice in grief.

Seven years go by. Dante's star has
lost its luster. He talks his buddy Howell
into digging up the grave, pulling out the poems.
Surely there is something he can rescue,
among the damp and moldy pages.

His friend reports that, unlike the poems,
Lizzie is still porcelain, still as beautiful
as when she overdosed, her red hair laid out
like rays on a satin pillow, tangled like Ophelia's.
Rossetti doesn't care to paint this picture.

*The subject of this poem is Elizabeth Siddal (1829-1862), who had a
twelve-year relationship with the Pre-Raphaelite poet and painter, Dante
Gabriel Rossetti.*

Camille Claudel's Waltz in Bronze

Laura Altshul

Camille: chosen by Rodin to learn and earn
the title of sculptor: became also
muse and model and mistress
when young, so young: Auguste
verged to fall when she was spring.

He taught, she grew, some thought her talent
beyond him; they tangled and fought,
parted and returned, enmeshed in art and love.
She cast their lives in bronze—
lovers embrace in passionate dance.

He bends to her, one arm at her bare back
gripping as she swoons in almost fall—
his head on her shoulder, her head on his,
sinuously they lean, hands clasping, dangled
bodies captured in the musculature of the waltz.

He was her hold, yet he stayed true
to his wife and other young women,
spurned Camille as she blossomed
and swelled with life that she doomed,
her family estranged, her talent strangled.

They said she needed to be locked up.
But imprisoned in this sad state unable
to move and sculpt she floundered for years
a modern Niobe, all lamentation and tears
and anger until she died.

No body, no marker, no grave
only the measure of bronze saved—
lovers embrace in passionate dance.

Olga Confronts Modernism

Carmen Germain

"As for me, I have no fear of art," Picasso said.

But how was it when she first saw *The Bathers*,
the concave yellow of his lover's hair,

how every oval offered a vagina, every
cabana the Minotaur's lair?

Near salt water, the sun
spread its red scarf

on a giantess and her sisters, thighs
massive as pylons of a wharf,

and from a mirror of many colors,
a girl with a belly of moon gazed at a man.

You can paint with whatever you want—
hooks and nails. The hearts of women.

*As his wife, Olga was used by Picasso to keep himself unattainable and safe
from any marital hopes his serial Muses might have entertained. The reference
"concave yellow" refers to one of these mistresses, Marie-Thérèse Walter, who
was seventeen when Picasso was drawn to her. He often referred to himself as a
Minotaur.*

Haunting the Hemingway House

Esther Whitman Johnson

They called the first *The Paris Wife*.
The third, famous in her own right,
was a glamorous romp in the hay.

Mary, the last—long-suffering bore—
was with him at the end, picked up
pieces till there was nothing more

to mend. She's the one who found
him dead, a bullet in the head, I,
the second, fell through the crack,

the wife no one remembers. If not
for this house at the end of The Keys,
I'd be a mere footnote in history.

But I threw a punch straight to the
gut, got the bastard where it hurt.
While he screwed Gellhorn in some

foreign bar, I tore out the boxing ring
where he sparred with drunken pals
on boozy nights, replaced it with a

swimming pool, largest in The Keys.
When he returned—as he always did—
I handed him the bill, shockingly big.

Living well is the best revenge, they wrote
of his Paris days, but Hem knew nothing
then of revenge or irony; for I still haunt

this tainted house, and every night it amuses
me to see the only female in his bed this time
is a six-toed feline named Gertrude Stein.

Of Hemingway's four wives, Pauline, the second, is probably the least well-known. Touring the Hemingway House in Key West, surrounded by the famous six-toed cats, I felt the spirit of Pauline everywhere and thought she deserved a voice, as well as a wicked sense of humor.

Ocean's Floor

Janet Joyner

> *Marie Tharp, 1920-2006*
> *Bruce Heezen, 1924-197*

Liebespaar? or not? is how
the thinking usually went;
for only Cupid's bow, unbent,
could pin a woman's heart
to stick, like a dart, to such a chart,
with such a man, is what was thought,
back then. And so the first to draught,
to map the sonar soundings
pinging depths to document
the Atlantic's rift, and shift
to proof of continental drift,
this quiet, steadfast, female heretic
who was content to just find
interesting work and not
lament her anonymity.
Yet it is said, that when he died,
she cut up his old clothes
and had them sewn, repurposed,
into skirts and jackets of her own.

*Marie Tharp was the American geologist and oceanographer who mapped the
ocean floor, forever changing scientific understanding of the planet. Ignored
and marginalized for much of her career, her story can be read in the award-
winning biography Soundings by Heidi Felt.*

After *High Noon*, Edward Hopper

Carol Frith

Shadows right-triangle the house, falling
across the dark door, the whitewashed clapboard.
That's Jo on the porch. Naked save for a blue robe.

But who was Jo? Jo, the wife who modeled when she
was not painting. Jo who painted, we're not sure what.
Not these shadows, right-triangle to the house.

Edward painted this. We know Jo painted trees in
every color of the spectrum. And faces, in the French
manner. Jo, half-naked here, on the porch.

It was Edward who painted her here, robe
falling open, breasts exposed in the naked light,
shadows in right triangles against the house.

But what did Jo paint? Herself, occasionally, aging
into the mid-light of the twentieth century.
That's Jo on the porch, half-naked in blue,

just where Edward placed her, breasts exposed.
I think I already mentioned that. That's who she was,
then? Shadows right-triangled against the house,
Jo on the porch, naked save for a blue robe?

*Josephine (Jo) Hopper, wife of Edward Hopper, was an artist in her own right
with a promising future at the time of her marriage. Though she continued her
work after marrying, her reputation faltered. She is best known now for having
served as model for many of Edward Hopper's paintings. Much of Jo's artwork
has been discarded or lost.*

Lee Krasner, Artist Forgotten

Sherri Bedingfield

She stood among trees painting a portrait of herself.
The mirror, secured against an opposite tree, offered reflection:
artist in a wood. Her easel on uneven ground,

she took her paints outside and proved herself to the Academy.
Few women did that in her day. An artist born to live her life
out loud renamed herself twice. From Lena, to Lenore,

from Lenore, to Lee. Then Lee for life.
A born artist, her colors spread wild across the air, across
huge canvases the world could witness.

*

When she married Pollock a tightness came to her face,
a mask with lines, stiff curves around her mouth. Pollock, brilliant bully,
his paint splattered in drunken rage. Something electric waited
under her tender skin. With him her paintings became slabs

of gray rectangles. He made her so tired. Her art reduced to dull bouquets
of flowers and vegetables, collections of unusual stones, garnet chunks,
hematite and smoky quartz she placed on window-sills.

*

She must have been cold in their cottage alone,
Pollock with his lovers. Did she think of children or pretend
future scenarios anyway? Stare at the ceiling past midnight?

When morning was a low white sky held up by tree tops,
did she stand in a haze, her back against a wall trusting and not trusting?
Leaning toward what, when? Did she hate, hate, hate?

*

After Pollock, she became a changing portrait herself. She took
her paints outside again. Did she find a fitting place, a level ground
to create her own space?

*This poem touches on a dynamic many, many intelligent and talented women
have experienced. That is, putting their work, art, priorities, and self-care aside
to promote their husband's or partner's, even if their husbands or partners are
unkind or abusive to them.*

Making Herstory

The Testimonial of Virginia Dare

Alison Townsend

I.

Our colony – the one I was named for – went silent
before I could speak. But I remember my mother's arms,
the sweet blue taste of her milk, the firelight, the forest
and faces around me, everyone's hopes pinned on a child
carried across the sea in her mother's heaving belly.

The shape of who I was and what I might have been
disappeared like the tracks we left in sand on the island,
gathering mollusks and driftwood, a beach swept clean
every morning, my story the country's first white myth,
my life a blank page awaiting invention's pen.

Blond-headed child dressed in buckskin and shell;
a white doe shot by an Indian to reveal my human form;
the vine that sprang up where the white deer fell, my fruit
sweeter than any before, my juice red as blood – scuppernong,
the grape from which the first new world wines were made.

II.

Say I was taken, my life remade among kind people
with skin only a few shades redder than mine with whom
I led an entire life on an island a few miles away. Or say
I simply vanished, a girl shape stitched into the mind
of a country the world hadn't yet imagined.

Say I was silence before it was a word, a dreaming
before it found pictures and form. Say I was a river of stars
that led to the sea. I was hush, I was sap, I was wanting, a bird's
twitter, the bee's golden hum of pollen. Say I was a body,
a twist of mewling sinew. Say I was hunger and bone,

the white flower that bleeds when picked. Say I was learning,
and then forgetting, and learning again, my bare feet wet
on the cold shore where I built a tiny village in the sand from memory.
Say I was what lay ahead, stretching west across our island
in the bay to the mainland, all the forests of America

waiting, wild-green, unplundered, heart of everything
a woman might be. Say I was a girl who became that woman,
resilient as a feather in the ocean-washed wind, my arms
wrapped around me for comfort, pearls in my shells'
moonlit interiors reflecting a self sieved through time.

III.

Like the beach sand in my grandfather's hand when he finally
returned and found us gone, each beloved grain trickling
back, lost to him, indistinguishable among the many,
but shining up like jewels, a part of me everywhere,
all of me nowhere, my name – Virginia Dare –

so like daring or courage, flung down here,
on this island where I was last seen alive, a riddle of arrival
this country is still trying to solve, loneliness my other name,
coupled with absence and longing, the echo of all
I was written in sand and water.

What really happened – who can say? There are a thousand
possible stories, the undiscovered country waiting between us,
another ocean's waters shining three thousand miles away.
America, America, I am the red brand burnt in your heart.
Begin with what disappears; live with of how you go on.

*Virginia Dare, first English child born in America, vanished without a trace
with the rest of the Lost Colony of Roanoke, circa 1587-1590.*

Contemplation

Dianalee Velie

> *This mean and unrefined ore of mine*
> *Will make your glistering gold but more to shine*
> —Anne Bradstreet

Subservient to God and man,
you praised in prose and poems
their stellar flare and the love
you felt beyond compare.

Yet in this burning, great desire
to shout their praise,
your flame flickered brightest
your need to write untamed.

With pen in hand you roamed
the forest and stoked your hearth
seeing God in every cricket and ash,
and love of husband, pure, unmasked.

A survivor of exile and loss,
you made this land your own,
telling a Puritan woman's tale
in verse to verify your vision.

And so your words drift
down through the centuries,
the first woman poet
published in a proud new land
master mentor, model and marvel.

Grace Sherwood, *Witch of Pungo*, Advanced in Age

Renée Olander

Indeed they called me a *beauty*—not that you'd see a trace
at my age, but in all my days I never had a wart,
                                        neither
did I keep it secret I could find receipts for cures—
some teas of roots and herbs—
                            rosemary, willow-root, ginger,
mint—too many to name, heaven knows. And I had liked
to entertain, and to talk, whatever the topic of the day—
                                    a quality
unbecoming to my sex, some still like to say, but I
had rather be tied than hold my tongue when wronged and then
it was one thing after another—
            Any spot could be mark of the Devil they said,
and despite my once fair face I admit divers moles and
childhood scars—
                    as when they stripped me, they saw:
spider veins, webbed toes, the palest pink skin:
                                    Mama had called me
her *little pig*.
            So when they hog-tied and tossed me into water,
well, I declare, the sky went dark almost as pitch and every soul
grew quiet. Now it's called *Witch Duck Point*, where that crowd
just cheered me on to drown—
                            yet I knew the wet hemp
would loosen, and I surfaced.
                            Despite the eight years'
hardship in their cell, I found a few kindly souls to call friends,
and outlived most of them who said I kilt their cows
and hogs.   I curst them.   I learnt a few spells.

Grace Sherwood was tried by dunking in 1706, condemned as a witch, and jailed for eight years. In 2006, she was exonerated by Virginia Governor Tim Kaine.

May 17, 1720: Superiour Court Justice Counsels Elizabeth Atwood in His Chambers Before Sentencing Her to Hang

Vivian Shipley

If any woman be delivered of any issue of her body, male or female, which, if it were born alive, should by law be a bastard and that she endeavor privately, either by drowning or secret burying hereof, or any other way either by herself or the procuring of others, so to conceal the death thereof that it may not come to light, whether it were born alive or not, but be concealed, in every such case the other so offending shall suffer death as in case of murder, except such mother can make proof by one witness at the least that the child whose death was by her so intended to be concealed was born dead.
  —Massachusetts Provincial Laws, 1692–93, Chapter 19, Section 7.

In the final conversation about Judgement, you will be the first
to get to give your version. Quivering to hear your name,

Elizabeth, remember scarlet in the live oaks was blinding
that first day when the bench you sat on was just a bench.

Hair thin as dune grass, I believed I had roots, that your beauty
would not be small waves coming in with the tide, sucking

my clothes. I left, came back. Left, came back, hiding under
branches so God would not see me, thinking how cool, green

the garden must have been. Michael Wigglesworth, I wrote
in my diary, *For admiring myself, I loathe myself.* Your house,

a whistle only I could hear, the gray cat was the other life I saw.
Pressing my stomach against your spine, your breasts cupped

in my palms were better than any hope of afterlife. I fell asleep
in your bed, awakened to a gull startling me like a rusty hinge.

Fog hung like a bedsheet. I was in the wrong house, could not
find my clothes, my wife. The first time, I told her I had been

praying deep in briar, then it was the bay gleaming like tar,
the smell of the Atlantic that drew me. Those dawns spread like

a rash, but sunset was your menstrual smear until there was snow
filling, white, white, swelling to banks. I never wanted the child

to be the sum of our parts, rounded into an irregular face almost
human. Even under oath, I knew you would not name me father.

This court will never prosecute me for fornication or adultery.
Our bastard's red hair above my earlobes would have spoken

our sin in each street of Ipswich. You refused to kill what love
had created. I had to do what you should have done. Surely,

Elizabeth, you must want to leave me in peace. When we go out
of this room, it will be time for you to say what you have to say.

The courtroom stilled by our entry, even God will be looking
down with interest. Like ships dry docked in Salem's harbor,

or dogs with heads cocked, Essex County's women are hushed
to hear loneliness, hurt, a poem you might have written. Spinster,

twenty-eight, you slept with no husband's arm across your hip.
Ipswich's men understand you were filled with sin, with desire.

I am trying to give you a defense. Plead insanity or great
emotional stress during pregnancy. Crazed by pain, you didn't

know what you were doing. Whisper ignorance, delirium,
or illness at birth. All are legal excuses for fatal neglect. Fitting

the weak nature you share with all women, claim inexperience.
Because of incessant crying, you dropped our son or placed him

in an unheated attic, fell asleep and had no money to pay for
a doctor. You could have overlaid such a small body, smothered

it in bed. Just last year, I acquitted an exhausted mother because
her infant slipped from her unsteady grasp, fell into the privy.

Using gloves, I was careful, didn't leave marks on our son's neck
to condemn you. No recorded testimony, the boy was

already dead when your stepmother came and cleared herself
by giving this court the date of birth. February the 20th is branded

into me. Willful, unrepentant, you wear your blood-stained dress
to court, but will not acknowledge your sin. Elizabeth, how can

I save you? Don't ask me for what purpose and quote St. Paul,
I Corinthians 15: *Flesh and blood cannot inherit the kingdom.*

Ink dripping from my pen, you give me no choice but to date
your death warrant: June 23, 1720. As the chief magistrate

for Massachusetts Superiour Court of Judicature, Assize and
General Goal Delivery, it's my duty to lead you to Mile Lane

and High Road, watch Sheriff Denison hang you at gallow's lot
on Pingrey's Plain. Elizabeth, raise your clenched hand to me,

uncurl it slowly, release me at least from your judgement. Think
of my days closed up in this room after you are gone. Imagine

the ache in my lungs, like a right whale wheezing in dark, each
breath in deep water held a very long time. Spring will resurrect

our first mornings. I will peer from attic slats, not knowing one day
to the next, if I will stride around a judge, vivid like God,

shoulders in the clouds or be staring into that little elastic face.
If I take a walk into a pasture, the scent of milk on your breasts

might come to me. Think of the place in my body where the past
with you will thorn, rise sharp as the question of what will

happen to me if I am found out. Sins deducted from graces,
you will go to heaven, but I will be roped to this earth, knotted

by memory, by the fear of last breath: the noose on your throat,
my hands like a baptism chain circling the neck of our son.

The Census Taker

Tina Egnoski

> *We entered the River Styx gently. Surely, death itself must come as quietly.* —Marjorie Kinnan Rawlings, Cross Creek

On horseback we set out at dawn. Zelma counts
the living, black and white.
I count vultures. Sparse
shadows, circling. Our mares keep track
of cottonmouth coils
like pie tins half buried in earth.

We trundle pine prairie and hammock dense
with hickory and bay. Cypress swamp—musty peat-meat.
Horse hocks part the river lilies, cattails graze
our shins.

My companion, raucous and lousy-mouthed,
knows every hoof-step
of this backwoods scruff, every local. Tick mark
for turpentine and moonshine stillers, women
with children on lap and at chest. Farmers, square
dancers, story-seers. The migrant and the tenant. Tick,
tick. Squatter, sitter, wagon driver. Tick for outlaws,
tick for in-laws. Hunters, maids, cooks, weavers, fishers, fence
menders, dress menders. Tick for father
teaching son to skin a coon. Tick for worshipers, grove
men, gas siphoners, milkers,
nurses, drunkards, sugar cane grinders. Tick, tick,
tick until the pad is black with lead.

We turn for home, breach again the river. A heron
wades—white spectral in mourning
hood. We cross and live
to tell tales of the living,
of the living and the alive.

Marjorie Kinnan Rawlings moved to Cross Creek, Florida, in 1928. She fell in love with the pine scrub country and the people who lived there. In the fall of 1930, Rawlings went with her friend Zelma Casson to take the census of backwoods Alachua County. The only way the women could reach many of the remote places was on horseback.

Matilda Lawrence

Mary Makofske

1.
Lights flee across water as she steps off the boat
in Ohio, and thereby declares herself free.
Free to hide, go hungry, live like a thief.
Darkness a cloak around her till she gathers
courage, walks in daylight down a street.
No more than glances. No rough hands seize her.
Doesn't the very air caress her? Here's a notice—
how glad she is she can read! Free, free to work
for wages in the house of a man who doesn't
question her history. History she can no more shed
than she can shed her honeyed skin.

Honey, her father all but said, you are so lucky.
Lucky you can pass for white. Lucky I own you.
You don't bend in fields under a hot sun.
You don't get bred to a coarse man
black as night. Nights I come to you,
I treat you like the treasure that you are.

2.
Silence. I know its value. Said nothing when master
offered a trip to Cincinnati, word that made
my heart leap. Said nothing when he whipped
the slave whose eyes flicked at me. Said nothing
when Mr. Birney asked if I'd ever kept a house.
Just nod, I told myself. Just nod my thanks
when he hands me wages I count in my own
small room where no one enters without my say.

3.
I polish silver, catch dust before it lands,
make beds as if a king might rest his dreams there.
Catch Mr. Birney's eyes on me now and then, not
lusting, but curious. I dream there is no
past, but I can't dream a future.

A door cracks open, men gambling
in a smoky room, but not for money.
That fierceness I recognize. That drive to win.
Abolitionists, the men our masters
warned us to beware. Why do they risk
their own lives for our freedom?
Mr. Birney's press smashed, the crowd
shouting at his front door, waving torches.
Young Mr. Birney standing on the steps
to turn them back. Lord, Lord, I did not
know what house I entered here.
The words that churn inside these walls
blaze up and frighten even me.

4.

I heard they were singing and dancing,
wild as anyone to celebrate Independence
Day, but it made the white men crazy.
They would not share their freedom.
They would not let those Negroes
elbow in beside the saints who signed
the Declaration, yet held slaves.
Try to take our fireworks and music,
you'll get fists and clubs and bullets—
that's what the white men say.

5.

One night I wake to screams I didn't hear
and smell the ashes of the homes
I didn't lose. Their dark bodies flee
to hide like animals in the woods.
The white men call us savages,
but it is they who riot through the streets
of Cincinnati. I try to tuck the nightmare
of their hatred in the past.

But today, one spit on an old Negro
sunning himself by the dock.
What had that old man done?
What had he done but live?

6.
I see them in the streets, the kidnappers,
can tell them by their keen eyes fixed
on colored skin, even on skin as light
as mine, on faces they try to match
with images of slaves the owners want back.
Don't stare, I tell myself, and no stare
lights on me, my respectable clothes,
the bonnet that shades my face.
I curse and bless the skin that masks me
from such scavengers. Once a slave,
what can it mean to be free?

Agitation. What Mr. Birney and his friends
stir up. What it stirs up in whites
who hate all Negroes, hate their own
who take our part. Agitation. What grips
me like a fever, trips the rhythm of my heart.

7.
And when it comes, the rough hand on my arm,
hasn't dread gripped me a dozen times before?
Don't I know to fight is of no use?
Haven't my night terrors
shown me more times than I can count
this cell, these bars, these voices cursing me?

Don't fret, says Mr. Birney. Salmon Chase
knows the Ohio statutes like his name.
It's a shaky raft I cling to—words on paper,
words that can be changed, or wrung
to mean what they were never meant to say.
I am ashamed to bring this trouble
to a man so kind. Mr. Birney now is charged
with harboring a slave. No, says Mr. Chase.
Everyone who treads Ohio's soil is free.

8.
Never sat in a courtroom before.
Never faced a judge with black robes
and a countenance like a bloodhound.

Mr. Chase rises and hurls in the air words
that wing past me like birds. I recall that poem
he loves, three lines of it I keep:
Slaves can not breathe in England; if their lungs
Receive our air, that moment they are free:—
They touch our country, and their shackles fall.
But I'll never step ashore in England.
Ohio is a free state, but its air can't
set me free. I cannot get my breath.
Shackles chafe my wrists. Lawrence
points a finger to name me his.

9.
At our last meeting, Mr. Birney begs
my pardon. I should beg his. Look how
they make him pay for hiding me—a fine of $50!
He is not guilty, or at least I think he's not.
Am I? "What offense has she committed?"
Mr. Chase demanded. "For what cause
is she imprisoned?" I thrilled to his words,
they seemed so true. Yet I blushed with shame.

10.
Lawrence stands in shadows to see her off.
So they were right, his friends who swore
you couldn't trust the best of them.
Slaves have no gratitude, no loyalty.
He didn't want her back, the little hussy.

Bound below deck, she knows where she is bound.
New Orleans, where she'll fetch a pretty penny
and earn her keep with a body all too fine.
She sways with the roll of the great river, a braid
of streams running down from where they were born.
Where she was born they said *Your life is charmed,*
though it flowed from a poisoned spring.

She won't see home again, if home
it was. She won't see again the father
who made and the master who un-made her.

These events took place 1836-1837. Salmon P. Chase, later a member of Lincoln's cabinet, defended Birney and argued Matilda could not be considered a slave in a free state (Birney vs. Ohio). Birney appealed and his fine was struck down. What happened to Matilda after she was sent to New Orleans is unknown.

The lines quoted are by British poet William Cowper (1731-1800).

Call Our Names

Nancy Clarke Otter

They call me Jane Davis
so that must be my name.
I came out of Caroline County
over to New Market, Cabin Creek,
on the Eastern Shore.
In the life I came to live
I asked for only two things:
First, when I was whispered to be sold South,
I asked for the strength
to make free, and I did.
I can't tell you how old I was,
but I had the change of life already
maybe 10, 12 years back.
Second, before I died
slavery should end,
and it did
maybe ten years after I came up
here to St Catharines.
Now I am dead I have
one more thing to ask:
speak my name,
speak our names, speak
Samuel Green and John Pinket,
speak Sara Jane Bell from Kent County.
Speak some each night and each morning,
speak the names of we
who cupped all our whole lives
here in the little hollows of our own hands
and walked away,
we the living breath of liberty,
we the blood-song of self-will,
speak we whose hands touched
the tethered faces of liberty and death,
call our names, call Elizabeth Banks from Easton,
Henry Osborne out of Seaford,
George Nelson Washington of Queen Anne County,
Sarah Elizabeth Roberts from Perryville,
William Griffin from Cambridge,

James Henry Watson, Snow Hill,
Sarah Catherine Young out of Kent County,
Josiah Stanley, Dorchester County,
Harriet Shephard and five children from Chestertown...

Names, including Jane Davis's, as well as towns, counties, and notes on who was left behind are all from William Still's The Underground Railroad. *Thousands more can be found in his records. Still's parents and siblings were among many enslaved people who escaped from the Eastern Shore of Maryland prior to the end of the Civil War.*

1842: US Army Expedition—58 Days, 85 Soldiers, One Native Guide, One Woman

Karla Linn Merrifield

My Seminole husband,
your guide, earned a pittance
and I earned

no thanks
for my crane liver stew,

no thanks
for mending mosquito netting,

no thanks
for salves to soothe
sunburn, sawgrass gashes,
and poisonwood rashes,

no thanks
for sucking cottonmouth venom
from puncture wounds,

no thanks
when you took my brown womanhood
by force.

I, *Aw-won-aw Hoke-tee*,
Willow-Tree Woman,
who once bent to white men, I say:
No thank you.

*All that historians know of this woman is recorded in a brief footnote (in
9-point type): a nameless "Seminole woman" accompanied the troops that year
into the unforgiving Everglades. As a poet waxing herstorical, I felt ashamed,
and wrote this cameo to give her a name and imagine her flesh-and-blood
story that had never been told.*

Eulogy

Vernita Hall

"Praise the Lord!" —Rebecca Cox Jackson, on being told of the death of her brother, Reverend Joseph Cox, former pastor of Bethel

1843

My only father, my delinquent teacher,
my sun. I fought to follow you, the preacher.
To serve my Lord as I served you, with all
my spark. You knew I heard the trumpet call.

They published* me, and witnessed me a witch;
threatened me with stoning, as heretic;
called me "high-sensed," proud, a self-named prophet.
A word from you, my brother, could have stopped it.

I raised eight children—none of them I bore—
without complaint. Six of them were yours.
You bade me pour your coffee out
You saved me poor, then cast me out

You think that death will balm the branded hurt?
Yes, I forgive—now pour yourself   some dirt

* banned from preaching

Black Philadelphian Rebecca Cox Jackson (1795-1871) overcame illiteracy, fear of thunder and lightning, and determined resistance to her calling to preach in the early African Methodist Episcopal Church (women were denied ordination) to become an itinerant minister and a Shaker Eldress. Fueled by her visions and her "gifts of power," she founded an order of black Shakers in Philadelphia.

Six-Horse Charley Parkhurs

CB Follett

No barroom brawls for me, no late
nights, no kisses sweet in the moonlight.
But they say I am the best damn
driver—four in hand, six-up,
eight. Want your fancy folks to
get there safely? Want your pretty
golden nuggets to reach the assayer?

Go to Mountain Charley they say. Even
Wells Fargo hired me to get
all that gold across the plains and rivers,
through The Badlands, out the back side,
from one ocean to another.
Good with a pistol, a rifle, a bull whip,
yeah, keep off you rough robbers,
you Blackfeet, you Sioux, Charley's
coming through like a hot knife through butter.

A top stage driver is a thing of beauty.
Horses matched and harnessed,
pulling stride for stride, dust rising
off the trail into clouds. I knew the routes
like they was printed on my arm:
Rough and Ready, Grass Valley, Poker
Flats, Placerville, all the gold towns were home.

Knew the sinkholes, where stage robbers
thought they could layby and take me.
Only worked once, never again. I rode
on through, reins in one hand, pistol
in the other and my rifle as a seatmate.
Yeah I shot Sugarfoot. Plain foolhardy
to rob me a second time.

I didn't expect to get away with it,
not for long. Now I've been
driving the stages for years, breaking
horses, binding my breasts
flat every morning,
every evening, sweet release.

I was young Charlotte when they died—
me and my brothers got fostered out.
First of many a bad scene in my life.
Already had short hair to keep off
the vermin, so, I took a set of Jack's clothes,
and his second best boots and lit out.
Only eleven, but getting taller by the day.

Worked the stables, always moving
west until there was no more west
but water. Even when Old Pete kicked out
my eye. I never held it against him, spooked
as he was by a rattler as I was fixin'
to attach his new shoe. Didn't
stop me, why should it. Rode on—
One-Eyed Charlie now—
wearing a black patch like a pirate.

Only once did I get caught out.
So cold, so cold, as I waited for my fare
to finish fancy dancing, my hands got
frostbit. I couldn't drive the horses.
Someone got me back to Mrs. Clark—
half dead of it, and she sent her boy in
to fill me a hot bath and get my clothes off.
Well, he saw it all, and he told his Maw,

"That there Charley's a woman." But they
kept my secret—bless 'em for that.
And it weren't never revealed until
my autopsy. Even my pregnancy.
Wonder what they thought
of the tiny red dress and baby shoes
at the bottom of my battered old trunk.

By then, what did I care?
It just boosted up my reputation.
They'll never take that away from me,
Old Cockeyed Charley, Best
Whip of the West.

Charley Parkhurst (1812–1879) was a well-known stagecoach driver during the gold rush period in California and beyond. She was the first woman to vote in the USA (1868), though no one knew it at the time.

Victorian

Elise Hempel

They held an umbrella in the sun
for Mary Surratt, shading her face,
making sure she didn't burn
before they fit the hood and noose,
and bound her skirts so as not to offend
the crowd as she fell in a last quick wind.

*Mary Suratt, who was hanged on July 7, 1865, for her supposed involvement
in the assassination of Abraham Lincoln, was the first woman executed by the
United States government.*

Cherokee, NC 1878

Teresa Poore

They named her Savage.
And when I say they named her Savage,
I don't only mean that they called her that,
although they did.

I mean that the bill of sale the white men
gave my Scottish great great-grandfather
so he could leave the reservation with her in tow
read, First name: Margaret, Last name: Savage.

I mean that if she had been
my great great-grandfather,
my name would be Savage.
          So be careful

when you touch me
you touch a wild thing.
I mean to say this flank is feral:
I am Teresa, a savage.

Margaret Savage was my maternal great great-grandmother. Her story has been handed down, as oral history, in my family for over five generations.

On the Last Day When No One Was Looking

Catherine Keefe

for Maria Spelterini

You test
what is taut. First
bare step cold as wind wire
whistle. Voice across calls. Falls, fall like no silent
thunder. Below bellows. Above roar mist, a rainbow
palette. Azure blur. Not all those on edge
expect you to soar. One second. Pure
spirit lights. A kick-split. Aloft. Alone you
exalt mid-air. Leap higher than heavenward.
Eyes carry a dream. Cross all void.

Oh!

Void all. Cross-dream a carry. Eyes
heavenward, then higher. Leap mid-air. Exalt!
You alone aloft. Split-kick. Alight Spirit.
Pure seconds. One soars to you. Expect
edge on those, all not blurred azure. Palette
rainbow. A mist roar above bellows. Below, thunder.
Silence knows like fall. Falls call across voices. Whistle
wire, wind as cold. Step bare
first-taught is what
tests you.

*Maria Spelterini became the first woman to cross Niagara Gorge on a tight
rope, July 8, 1876. She's the only woman to ever accomplish the feat. She
crossed three more times, once blindfolded, once wearing peach baskets on her
feet, once with her hands and ankles shackled. Her last crossing was on July 26,
1876.*

The Lucky Pillow of Annie Edson Taylor

Julia Paul

My kitchen table had a book under one leg
to keep it from collapsin' the rest of the way.
I'd sit with the newspaper spread like a map
across it. That's when the idea hit me.
Them Niagara Falls is just waiting for me.
I'll be the first.

Lost my husband to the Civil War,
been widowed almost forty years.
Can't remember his face or what it feels
like being loved. The struggle to support
myself started and ended my days.
Fame and fortune is what I craved.
Get rich quick and live on easy street.

Fame and fortune. Fame and fortune.
How sweet it'd be!
A barrel and some luck. Why, seems
I'd be needing my own bank to hold
all the money. I'll be smart. Get me a manager.
Lie about my age, tell them I'm 43,
not 63. Still got my figure after all them
years teaching dance, don't you know.

Lined the barrel with pillows.
Sewed them myself—heart shaped
for luck. Wasn't too scared. Either way
it turned out I'd be escaping my
rotten situation. That's how I figured it.
Got to be honest, I loved all the attention.
All them New York Times reporters
hanging around. The mayor.

I know some people came to watch me fail.
Took bets on how many pieces the barrel'd
be in when it was over.
I prayed for them right along with myself
when I started rolling along. It was dark
as night inside. Figured that's what death
is like. Darkness everywhere and no way out.

Almost twenty minutes, the thunder
of the water told me I was nearing the Falls.
I was in God's hands when I went over.
Don't remember that part t'all.
When they took me out of the barrel—
well—I had me two thoughts: First
was hallelujah. Second was no one
ought ever do that again. Tussy Russell,
my manager, done run off with the money.
My barrel, too. Chicago is where
we found the barrel.

*On October 24, 1901, Annie Edson Taylor became the first person ever to
successfully go over Niagara Falls in a barrel.*

1887: Annie Oakley Is Done

Susan Terris

Done. Done. Done. Such a stick-in-the-mud when flanked
by me. At 26, she's old. No flair. No style. A midget-woman.
Not big and comely. See, I have a fine face, bouncy

bosoms, swell-swivel hips, whereas that done-woman,
an apple-pan-dowdy, has the same shape as her gun.
And I, just 15—I get the misters, the prizes,

the fame. See my ruffle-busting clothes, my pretty feet.
I'm a trick rider, too, in the ring—and on a mattress.
And I am a crack shot. Anything she can do, I can do

faster, longer, sweeter, hotter, better. Because of me,
she's history at Bill's Wild West thang. A ha-ha-hasbeen.
Gone today. Goner tomorrow. No one will remember

Annie. But every person in the whole effin' world will
remember and fall for me. Me: *Lillian Smith*.

*Last year, I came across a picture of Annie Oakley with her gun, and started to
research her & her life. Wild Bill Hickok really did hire young, beautiful Lillian
Smith to outshine Annie. For a while, she did. Then she didn't.*

Mistress Melody Brown, 1898

Susan Terris

You can call me Melody Brown—not my real name, of course,
any more than Oakley is hers. I am waiting with my weapon

and cache of munitions, because Annie has written President
McKinley a letter. And I am in it. Imagine me: plain and unmarried,

a lost Melody. But my time has come, because I am one of Annie's
(she taught each of us how to fire) 50 sharpshooter ladies.

Now we are on full alert for marching orders from our president.
My widowed momma would weep her way to church, cry

2 hankies if she caught wind of this. She taught me to cook and
can, to knit wool sweaters and make lace curtains. And she's not

yet done selling me. She's bee-in-a-bonnet for a widower with
children. Perish the thought, when I'm armed and hot to trot.

If or when we war with Spain, we shall all sail off to save
our country, adventurous, 50 strong ladies, with fierce

little Annie Oakley firing her shotgun and blazing the way.

*Annie Oakley did write President William McKinley in 1898 telling him she
had 50 lady sharpshooters armed and willing to fight for the U.S. This persona
poem is written in the voice of a "lady sharpshooter" I created. Check out the
photocopy of that letter from Annie: http://www.lettersofnote.com/2010/03/
fifty-lady-sharpshooters-await.html*

Letter from Antoinette Bope to Her Sister Mabel, May 24, 1902

Sue D. Burton

for my great-aunt Nettie, 1880-1902

Oh, Mabel, *that*
that I feared.
         Questions
loosed & plaguing me at night.
I wish to tether them & my body
that demands I touch
certain parts.
         Could it be the Soul
has like demands, for all Eternity?

'Spose God would look down
& say I have Sinned. Though Mac   ,
claims Sin's not
a constant.

But it all went so fast.
& the Truth is—
         writing
this morning makes
the letterpaper qualmy.

Papa would not approve
as Mac is not
prosperous
& not a Lutheran.

*

Have found a Mrs. Beatty.
Rickety stairs up & up,
five pine chairs & a picture of Jesus.

She poked my belly through my dress
& took my money & said, come back
on the morrow—

*

Mabel, the morrow
is upon me.

All night, dreamt of the Terrible Shooting—
& who would be next, when even the President
can't be kept safe?
I don't like to think about Death.

*

   Clock,
Unwind: be New Year's again—
today Unsuspected, Mac still
a glimpse, curly
black hair in need
of a trim,
bit of a lisp.

Oh, that my face were not
so broad & plain.

Fear, I am dizzy.

God has slacked
his Grip.

*

   Rickety Stairs, railings
corded with rags, have
Mercy on me.

(Yet how can Sin be raveled from the Soul?)

Mrs. Beatty has a chipped
tooth. Though my landlady says—
oh, by all accounts, she's—

if only—but, Mabel,
what *other*?

Always,

Antoinette Bope was my maternal great-aunt, 1880-1902. She is one of the many women who have died of illegal (secret) abortions and have been forgotten not only by society at large, but often by their own families.

The New Woman

Anne Harding Woodworth

> *I think [bicycling] has done more to emancipate women*
> *than anything else in the world.—Susan B. Anthony, 1896*

I want to be Annie Kopchovsky
and ride a bicycle around the world,
discard my bustle and petticoats,
my corset—and rescue the flex of my ribs,
find dance in their marrow.
I'll wear bloomers of twill. You see?
I too have two legs to bestride a Columbia frame.
I'll balance on a saddle and dig into handlebars.
I'll make money, carry a placard that proclaims
to the world the goodness of lithia waters.
I'll pedal with the wind. I'll pedal against the wind.
And my music will come with me.

*Annie (Londonderry) Kopchovsky (c. 1870-1947) rode a bike around the
world, advertising Londonderry lithia water, which was thought to be
therapeutic for kidney health. The company asked her to change her name to
Annie Londonderry.*

Eunice Winkless's Dive into Pool of Water: Pueblo, Colorado, July 4, 1905

Jeff Worley

It's the beauty of gravity, the solid
pleasure of falling she's
feeling above the packed
grandstands, halfway to earth from
the rickety scaffolding
one hundred fifty feet
in the air, riding the broad bare
back of this incredulous
stallion who tucks his forelegs
into his chest, having no choice
but to trust the stupid
ex-rodeo grifter clutching
the black shock of mane
as if determined to take
the whole whooping crowd with
her, make them never forget
that she was here, aiming
the horse toward the small
still target, Eunice's
legs rising
from the horse's ribs
as it picks up speed, Eunice
believing—again believing—
bones are lighter
than air, water will open
its arms, take her in,
push her out and up to the cheering world.

The diving horse act was allegedly started by Dr. W.F. Carver in the late 1880s while crossing a partially collapsed bridge on horseback. As both rider and horse plummeted, the horse dove straight into the waters below, inspiring Carver to develop a "diving horse act." Eunice Winkless agreed to do a horse-dive as a dare for a $100 prize and successfully dove headlong into a pool of water. She and the horse, according to legend, were not hurt by the stunt. However, Winkless was forced to sue to receive her $100 prize money.

The Rope and the Biplane: Edith and Wilbur

Renny Christopher

October 7, 1908

You can see it clearly in the photo of her
beside Wilbur there in the Wright Flyer—the rope
tied round her legs, just below the knee, to keep her
skirt from flying. That is, to keep her long skirt from
keeping her from flying, which she so much wanted,
she had to tie herself up.

But the bonds were worth it to escape the ground and
soar, even if only for two minutes, even
if only beside that blank faced man, even if
only while wearing a corset that kept her from
gathering the sky into her lungs, even so
it was delicious, to be the first of her kind
to be carried aloft by a self-propelled craft
so fast, so high, so far, beyond the reach of her
family, her husband, of her position in
society although not beyond the reach of
propriety so that even soaring, drunken
with the joy of one kind of freedom she must be
roped and on her face have no more expression than
the peculiar man who held the controls.

*Edith Berg was the first American woman to ride as a passenger in a
sustained powered flight, with Wilbur Wright. They flew for two minutes. The
first woman passenger in a powered flight was Therese Peltier, on July 8, 1908,
riding with Leon Delagrange. They flew 656 feet. In September of that year,
Peltier became the first woman to solo pilot a plane.*

Who Would Let a Black Girl Fly?

Lynn Veach Sadler

for Bessie Coleman, 1893-1926

Who would let a Black girl be?
Who would let a Black girl fly?

Taught herself to read.
Newspaper accounts of European air war
taught her to want to fly.

What flying school would teach a woman?
No flying school would teach *Black* woman.
Europe? More liberal toward women,
toward people of color.
"Bessie, study French!"
First licensed Black pilot in the world
via Federation Aeronautique International,
via Paris.
The Air? Only place free of prejudice.

Bessie would open flying school.
The Air: only place free of prejudice.
Bessie would teach other Black women to fly
with funding from flying exhibitions,
lectures on aviation.
"Brave Bessie" the papers called
stunt flying, barnstorming, parachuting
"Queen Bess"
in her war-surplus Jenny Trainer.
In air shows, air circus—
power dives, figure eight's, loops.
She refused to fly when Blacks were not
permitted through same entrances as Whites.
The Air would be the only place free of prejudice.

The day Bessie died, no seat belt, no parachute.
Bessie was thrown out.
Bystander's cigarette wrapped wreckage in flames.
Wrench found jamming controls.
The Air would be the only place free of prejudice?

Perfect Woman

Pat Mottola

> *They called me the "Diving Venus,"*
> *the perfect woman, a daughter of the gods.* —Annette Kellerman

Annette, it was 1907 after all.
You were arrested for indecency—
wearing a one-piece fitted bathing suit
on Boston's Revere Beach.
A "maillot pantaloon"—a unitard with no legs—
a suit that ended in shorts above your knees,
your legs causing a scandal, making you famous.

A professional swimmer, you lived
for the water, the first woman
to attempt to swim the English Channel.
It wasn't easy to do the crawl stroke
in pantaloons and a dress. You designed
your own line of suits, your own life,
spun away from the domination of men
that even today want to dictate what is
an acceptable place for women.

Annette, you were not *that* Annette, not
the Mouseketeer whose contract with Disney
insisted she be modest. Your sexuality key
to your vaudeville performances, your trademark
emphasized eroticism, form-fitting costumes,
a daredevil prowess. Advocate for women's
access to physical culture, you were met
with heavy resistance blocking your way
like a tidal wave.

Oh, Annette, tell them how in 1908, after a study
of 3000 women, Dr. Dudley A. Sargent of Harvard University
dubbed you the "Perfect Woman"—your physical attributes
closest to those of the Venus de Milo.

No no Annette, they wouldn't let you *attend* Harvard.
Those Ivy League men would study you
as if you were a textbook, key to their success.
Yet they barred their doors to your sex—to half
the population—until 1977. You were merely
a stepping stone in their Yard.
A silent film star, they didn't let you speak,
didn't give you a voice, tried to keep you silent.
But you were a screen siren. Even a star
on the Hollywood Walk of Fame.

You took off your clothes in 1916,
in *Daughter of the Gods*—
a lost film, no copies are known to exist.
Did those men intentionally try to erase you?
You didn't need men—you were a woman of substance.
Annette, there was nothing you couldn't do.
Uncredited "co-director" in this production, developer
of story lines, stunts, locations, and camerawork.

You scripted a death-defying waterfall dive. Fox
executives eliminated the scene—it looked
too risky. You mocked them, saying, "That's the way.
Somebody's always trying to take the joy out of life."

You refused a double for a scene that required you
to jump into a pool of crocodiles. You had experience,
Annette—those men you encountered on your way
up, men whose jaws would snap you in half
if you let them.

Dr. Sargent went to great lengths to research
perfect proportions of the human body, used his
Harvard connections to research subjects, collect
anthropometric data. But Annette, in 1918
you wrote the book. *Physical Beauty: How to Keep It.*

Song of the High Scaler's Wife

Heather Lee Schroeder

Clark County, Nevada, 1931

Look: milk curdles maggoty
in heat like this. Fruit shrivels;
babies stop crying. They gasp
like fish in a dry bucket—silent,
open-mouthed, miserable.
We eat no fruit, nothing fresh: nothing
but tins of mushy vegetables
and heat, intolerable:
filling up our bellies.

I tell him if I had known—
how he swings out from the rock, out
over oblivion, dangles for twenty-five cents
more an hour, writes his name
into history. There is nothing,
but dust and stone below.

Necks peel in ribbons
under sun like this. Hair turns white;
skin salty with sweat. We roast
like pullets on a spit—skin crisp,
dry and tender. We place wet cloths
over cradles, on super-heated limbs
and fontanels, tender: skulls
heating like eggs in a skillet.
Overhead no trees, no shade, no relief.

I say if I had only understood.
We left behind an orchard, timothy-rich pastures,
fat chickens scratching in the yard,
cows in stanchions, their bags heavy,
lowing for an evening milking,
tender brown eyes rolling in the socket.

I know how falling rock can kill the unwary
high scaler in an instant. Limbs tear
free; faces crumple under force. I have seen,
and I fear for him, like a rabid dog trembling

and mad for water and flesh.
I rock the baby outside our tent,
infant cheek sticky against my breast.
I have seen my husband, twisting
against the canyon wall, laughing.

I tell him if he has a heart, no—
but he lowers down anyway, tools jangling
on his waist, drills his holes, thrusts
dynamite into them and scrabbles away.
And I know: there is nothing
this man won't do for this dam.

Work on the Hoover Dam began in 1931 and continued through 1936, attracting more than 10,000 unemployed workers and employing some 5,000. Many of these men and their families lived in rough tent cities. Today, the workers who constructed the dam are celebrated, but they could not have completed their task without the support of the women who followed them to the site.

Yearbook Photo: Women's Rifle Team, Cornell, 1934

Mark DeFoe

I.

In white middies, pleated skirts, the team aims past
the nose of a girl smiling like Buddha. Far left,
another girl at parade rest, jodhpur clad,
letter sweater tight against her hips.
The wind billows her skirt. She smirks, hair curved
down near one eye. Between these assistant
the shooters sight. Behind them is a weedy bank.

II.

Slender forearms brace, hands cradle black barrels,
fingers caress—firing pins snap on nothing.
A barrel sags, a shoulder drops. Three times
they dry fire for this photo. Some wear heels,
and there's the sheen of stockings on their calves.
Their rank is neat. Cheeks nuzzling the walnut stocks,
some saw a target down the road—
a small bell they might ring, setting off parades.

III.

Most never fire again, thought one taught her son,
one when love-arched always cried "Bullseye."
Some dreamed of perforating diaper pails,
of winging husbands. But not that straight-backed girl
with the rock-steady rifle. In France, she watched
herself chamber a bullet. She locked in her stance,
emptied her mind, flicked off the safety,
and bisected, just down from his Iron Cross,
the tunic button of an SS captain.
Then let go her breath, seeing again in the faces
of those lost teammates, her only sisters.
Then let go her breath, tenderly
Took in the trigger's slack, and squeezed.

Sweeping

Jodi L. Hottel

Our battered suitcases stand by the door,
but they will have to wait
while I sweep away
the desert dust, one last time.

Three years we've lived
behind barbed wire.
Now, Papa and I are being forced out—
too old for farming,
no home to go back to,
our children already gone—
Sam to war in Europe,
a college in Chicago for Mei.

I pause in the doorway
of the barrack, our only shelter
from the bitter winds, dust-driven heat.
No need for a last look
at the sentinel of Heart Mountain.
It will never
be far enough away
that I can't see it.

I shove the broom hard
into empty corners, shaping
neat piles of sand.
Papa chides—
Why clean?
But I don't listen.

Whoever comes to demolish
these empty walls will see—
we Japanese kept our homes clean.

This poem is about an anonymous woman who is representative of many Issei, or first generation women, who were imprisoned in concentration camps for Japanese Americans during WWII. They were among the last people remaining in the camps because they had nowhere to go back to, as their property, homes and belongings had been taken from them.

Photo in Krakow

Elaine Zimmerman

She walks straight ahead.
A scarf covers her hair.
The chin angular, the eyes large.
Her hands push a carriage.
You cannot see the baby
but a child is resting.
Others walk before and behind her.
The clothes are brown or black.
She stands out.

She could be walking
to the bookstore or fruit market.
Who is she trying to fool?
Is the pace to confuse the child,
let her sleep a few more hours with
dreams of angels and sugar candy?
Or is she saying names of the living
to trick God into saving her?
This has sometimes worked for others.

Most look down.
She looks straight ahead.
Perhaps she sees someone she knows.
Someone must be ahead of her but
it does not appear so or maybe a
voice guides her to a different room.
She prays with her eyes open.

There will be no covered mirrors.
Water will not be spilled in every room
where death has dipped his dagger.
No one will walk a different path home
from the Vistula to keep death from returning.
There is only one path for now.

She will leave behind one ring and a
pair of brown shoes. Nothing else.
No one will close her eyes or
walk with her when she dies.
I close her eyes now but do not
know her name. It is never too late to
honor the dead and pray for the living.

I saw this mother in a Krakow photo. She could easily have been walking to a store with her child. But she was walking to her death. I felt compelled to stay as if something still needed to occur. It was the blessing for her departure that never took place. I said the Hebrew mourner's Kaddish and prayed for her in my own way. Then I could, reluctantly, leave her.

The Photograph in My Hand

Janet R. Kirchheimer

My mother, four years old, blond curls,
wearing a smocked dress, in a field of goldenrod,
her doll on her lap and her dog at her side.

Two years later, the girl in the photograph
would be backed up against a wall at school,
by kids in her class for refusing to say "Heil Hitler,"

and they would throw rocks, beat her up, call her *Jude*,
her dress would be torn, and her parents
would have to find a way to get her out of Germany.

She would be sent to an orphanage in Amsterdam,
and they would wait two years for their visas
to America. I want to ask the girl what

would have become of her if her parents hadn't
found a way out? Would she have survived?
Would she have been experimented on like her cousin Hanni

who returned home after the war and rarely
left her room, or would she,
like another cousin, Bertl, have tried to cross the Pyrenees

into Spain and never be heard from again? What if Hitler had never come
to power, would she and her parents still have come to America?
Would she have met my father, and who would

she have married if she had stayed in Germany, and
who would she have become and what would have become
of me? I cannot let go of it.

I was looking at the photograph of my mother and wanted to talk to that six-year-old girl and ask her so many things, especially who would she have been, and if she would still have been my mother if the Holocaust never happened. I also wanted to also honor two forgotten women, one experimented on and one killed.

Dear Tante Yvette

Pegi Deitz Shea

Your brother told me how brave
you were, at only 16, spying
in that Nazi collabo's office,

intercepting lists of Jews
in Paris to be rounded up,
and warning them to flee,

to follow you to the basement
and then down to the cellar and
then down further to the dirt floor

where the jackboots wouldn't stomp,
where you'd hidden food, blankets
and hundreds of Jews before,

or follow you to secret garages
where wagons waited to take them
to safe farms in Angouleme.

Please tell me:
How did it feel when they said,
"No"?
Certainement, les enfants?
"No."
Not even after you—panting,
bruised and bloody after running
from the boche who'd found you out,
raped you, beat you, left you for dead—
and you still came to their door
and begged them to flee?
How did that feel?

You said you'd left Paris
after the war because
there were too many ghosts.

Please tell me all
so you don't become
one more.

My brother married into a French family and his mother-in-law and her brother were teens in the French Resistance during WW2. I am working on a novel based on their experiences.

The Jar

Julia Paul

In memory of Irena Sendler, 1910-2008

Irena prints the name
on a slip of paper:
      Elzbieta Ficowska.
Yes, spelled correctly, she's sure.
Yes, yes. The child's mother
had repeated the letters for Irena
as she placed the baby into the box
while Irena secured the parcel
with brown paper and string.
The letters echo like a mantra:
      E-l-z-b-i-e-t-a....
The mother's breath caressed
each letter as if it were a tiny finger
wrapped around her own.

Irena drops Elzbieta's name
into the jar, slides the jar
behind rows of canned pickles
and cabbages. If the Gestapo
search, would they care what's
in a woman's pantry?

The confetti of names haunts Irena:
Gertrude, Heinrich, Hildegarde.
A slip of paper for each child
smuggled out of the ghetto.
A slip of paper for each child
taken from a mother's arms:
Franz, Dietrich, Gretel.
A slip of paper for each child
Irena's team carried out in packages,
carpenter's boxes, and laundry carts
during their rounds as sanitary inspectors.
A slip of paper for each child
delivered safely to a Christian family.

2500 slips of paper in a jar
on a shelf in a pantry
behind the pickles and cabbages.

Irena Sendler was a Polish nurse and social worker who is credited with saving the lives of 2,500 Jewish children after the German invasion of Poland. She and her co-workers entered the Warsaw ghetto as typhus inspectors and, at great risk to themselves, smuggled children out to be harbored by Christian families. The identities of the children and their parents were written on slips of paper and put into jars that were hidden in the hope of reuniting the families after the war.

Nurses of Bataan, Prisoners of War, the Third Year

Susan J. Erickson

Slowly starving,
our legs thinned to bamboo stalks
or swelled like palm tree trunks.

We and those we nursed
suffered anemia, beriberi, scurvy,
pellagra—the diseases of deprivation.

The lucky ones stopped menstruating,
saving us from the public task
of washing and drying homemade
fabric pads embroidered with our initials.

We ate okra and greens fried
in cold cream from Red Cross kits,
traded recipes rich in fat and calories,
planned fantasy menus.

Within the prison walls, sparrows,
pigeons, and cats disappeared. Thanksgiving dinner
was a ladleful of rice, a cup of vegetable stew
and a spoonful of *camote* tops.

Work was our meat of survival,
sunsets and moonlight our art.
Hope was a rag doll named Any-Day-Now,
in a uniform of khaki scraps,
liberated, too, when the gates crashed down.

*During World War II American nurses (Army and Navy) on Bataan Peninsula
were held prisoners by the Japanese for over three years.*

Paralysis

Janet Warman

> *Missy LeHand to Franklin Delano Roosevelt*

All the years in that chair,
your masquerade of health
was my life. I laughed
with you, hosted your parties,
indulged your stories, became
your partner in Eleanor's absence.
I was your ears in distant places,
your eyes in forbidden rooms.
"Give me gossip," you would say,
when what you wanted was for me
to make you forget your legs were stilled.

Now my limbs stiffen,
relegated to my own chair,
one day like any other,
news of the war from the radio
rather than from reading the press of your hand.
You can not spare a visit.
You can not spare a word
for your accomplice,
the one who made your eyes dance
when your legs were cold.

Marguerite "Missy" LeHand was secretary to Franklin D. Roosevelt and served as White House hostess when Eleanor could not be present. Their level of intimacy is uncertain. After a debilitating stroke, LeHand was devastated by her inability to continue to work for the president.

On the Map of Despair

Elena Lelia Radulescu

Maria, Safta, Rodna, Teresa, Jiva,
guilty for
being mothers and wives,
daughters and sisters to owners
of land, cows, horses, farmsteads;
guilty for
speaking more than one tongue,
as if words were silver bullets
meant to kill those of the new order;
guilty for
living close to the border, so close
some days they could hear the dreams
of their neighboring Serbs crying,
trapped onto the teeth of barbed wire.

Ana, Petra, Dabrinca, Mileva, Rada,
rounded up like lambs,
sentenced to a forced labor camp,
in the scorching fields,
north of the river Danube,
the new Siberia on the map of despair.

When the land entered
into the labor of spring,
hemorrhaging wild poppies far into the horizon,
side by side with their men,
Anca, Dejana, Flavia, Maranda, Liuta,
dug deep into the veins
of that parched ground,
forcing the water out,
quenching their thirst
but never the ache of their hearts.

Sofia, Pera, Nelia, Mitra, Lavina,
slaved, struggled and sweated
in the fields of tobacco,
corn, cotton, hemp and sunflower.
At night, they wove reeds into blankets
to cover their starved, cold bodies,
holding tight to their faith,
a rope thrown to their souls
by the God of exile.

Year after year,
Marica, Livia, Dobra, Pavlina, Anda
scattered seeds into the hard soil,
urging plants to bear life giving fruits,
cooked, raised children,
tended the old and the feeble,
buried the dead,
and slogged, toiled, worked
till the skin of their hands peeled
in strips like scrolls of papyrus,
blood inking the hieroglyphs
of endurance.

After five sweltering summers
the gales of history blew
Mara, Lisandra, Radva, Floarea, Ida,
to the old villages
at the foot of the mountains
back to their empty homes,
broken windows, glass shards on the floors,
sparrows nesting inside the cupboards,
roofless houses hosting
the rain, the snow, the wind.

Again, Stanca, Vlaha, Lana, Tita, Bora
began their work;
lit a fire, cooked a meal, raised a child,
plowed the fields, milked a cow,
sifted through their memories,
kept some, threw others away.

They lived with the past
in their hearts like a kernel
of wheat swaddled in the husk
of silence,
while the eye of the world
looked somewhere else.

On the night of June 18, 1951, 44,000 people from six villages on the Yugoslavian border were deported to the south east of Romania for security reasons.

Montgomery Bus Arrest: March 2, 1955

Laura Altshul

for Claudette Colvin

Before Rosa there was Claudette
sassy fifteen, she sat her ground
refusing to lift up and go back
for the white person demanding her seat
and the driver commanding her to leave.

She said she'd paid her fare
had the nerve to dare to stay
to fight for what is fair and right.
She'd studied Sojourner and Harriet,
brave souls who led the way.

Yanked up and out by two white cops,
school books flew from her lap.
They grabbed her skinny wrists,
cuffed and dragged and kicked her
and snarled vicious names.

Terror hit as the cell slammed shut.
She cried through her prayers.
She was the first to sit her ground.
Why Rosa? Why not Claudette?
Too young, too angry, too black.

Yet nine months
before Rosa she saw the way,
she was the way.

Elizabeth Eckford's Walk Toward Central High School

H.K. Hummel

September 4, 1957

Let no old woman spit on a girl.
Let no girl know the snarls
of a mob. Let a girl have more
to shield herself than gingham
and a pair of tortoise shell glasses.
Let a girl in tortoise shell glasses
know the ferocity of a hawksbill
tortoise. Let the city bus driver
be heroically prompt.

Let a girl remind us what shouldn't be,
yet sometimes must be, survived alone.
Let a girl know how to turn herself
into a crowbar, a library, a dogwood.
Let a girl be fifteen. Let her be called
Liza, or Lizzie, or Beth. Let a girl be.

Elizabeth Eckford was part of the Little Rock Nine, the first group of African American students to integrate Central High School in Little Rock, Arkansas after the Brown vs. the Board of Education of Topeka decision declaring desegregation unconstitutional.

Nicknames for Wilma Rudolph

Anne Champion

Soon, your older sisters began to smell sweet
with blood; the scent made the boys
sniff around them like police hounds. Soon,
you knew this would be your fate, so you unlocked
the metal braces, stayed after school and ran
the cinder track around the football field
for hours. It must have hurt at first, knowing
the limits of your body, your new skin
itching like a scabbed cut, like the dandelions
splitting the soil and pock marking
the lawn. At school, you learned to name
the world correctly—every country,
every species, every type of rock.
Which flowers will poison and which
to garnish your hair with. Your teachers never
uttered the names for dark skin,
never taught you where they came from,
because you all knew it in your veins; you could
deconstruct your pulses to know when
one meant lynching or one meant anomaly.
We called you The Tornado,
and you must have known we were afraid
you could destroy every foundation we've known.
We called you Black Gazelle, and you must have felt
your fangs grow, nourished by anger, hungry
to rip out the gut of the world that set
the records to break. The ones who admired
called you Black Pearl, stressing
how rare you were, how valuable, adorning
you around their necks for special occasions, proof
that Jim Crow didn't clip wings. You ran—
You ran until your bones felt brittle, until your muscles
wrapped around your skeleton like vines.

Whenever you crossed the finish line, you re-learned
the futility of escape, you re-learned that a circle
is infinity, that the track goes and goes
but the laps are only a temporary stay
against your permanent world.

*American Olympic sprinter, considered the fastest woman in the world in
the 1960s. Various countries had different nicknames for her, including The
Tornado, The Black Gazelle, and The Black Pearl. At age four, she contracted
polio and grew up wearing a brace a leg brace. She shocked everyone when she
removed the brace and walked unassisted at age nine.*

From Hulda Crooks' Journal

Carol Nolde

Hulda Crooks, the oldest woman to climb Mt. Fuji

When I was young, I wondered how I'd change
with age. I thought that growing old was growing
into someone else, but still I hoist
my pack on shoulders that are bent but strong
enough to carry food and gear, the burden
for the climb up Whitney when the weather's
good. The mountain's like a friend I need
to visit. I've learned its trees and shrubs by heart.
At first, I didn't know what lay ahead
but now the mountain's face is as familiar
as my own. No map can tell the roots
that rise above the ground, the pockets in rock
just right for hands to grip and haul the body
up, but like a friend whose moods I read,
I know the disposition of the land.

When people ask, do you still climb,
as if surprised I haven't tired yet,
I think of my retreat above the trees
where I watch hawks harness the breeze,
wings outstretched, carried motionless.
Like surfers propelled forward on waves, they float
until they feel the pull of earth, then pump
their way upward to catch another draft
to drift on. I bask on rocks, a lizard
not thinking of the climb ahead or back
or how the sun arcs the sky. I close
my eyes to the blue-gold day and the lakes
like shards of glass below and listen to the cry
of hawks and hear the beating of their wings.

*Between the ages of 65-92, Hulda Crooks climbed 14,000 foot Mt. Whitney
twenty-three times. At 91 years of age, she climbed Mt. Fuji.*

No Más Bebés

Ilene Millman

Life as an overcrowded city bus—
too many hands on the overhead bar,
too many hands: brown, worn, bare—
too many people who can't hold on.
Official papers hold fast their damaging account.
Best. Interest.
Words conjured from a silk hat
and the words flew out their fingers
like card tricks
and your bebés disappeared—
no use shouting,
the factory racket loud enough
to drown their lies.
Your husband
he already signed, they said—
their eyes filled with kindness,
when by this they meant
This one she has too many children—
the paper meaning nothing to you
until nothing turned its white mask of collusion
inside out.
It's late. A grandmother's regret
cannot wipe out the Yes,
the X on the line.
At the border
of sleep, what lights push against your eyes
what pulse sneaks under your heartbeat?

Dolores Madrigal and her husband worked in a factory to save money for a house and family. In the 1970s, doctors sterilized her and countless other Latina women during labor at the Los Angeles County Medical Center.

Christine Jorgensen Speaks to the Press

Anne Champion

There are two things that make a man feel powerful:
a cock and a gun. I had both. No sir, I never tended
any gardens, never nursed any sons, never let a man love
me so hard that he beat me until I was bitter and wise.
There's one thing that makes a woman feel powerful:
love. Loving is wonderful, but falling in love
is very stupid. I don't want to marry—even though
men hover around like hummingbirds at hollyhocks.
I'll never let one move in. My religion is to never
put a wild thing in a cage. I wasn't really ever a man,
so I never sowed a field, sir, never liked the way
a football wanted to be cradled like an infant,
never listened when they told me you could plant
grenades in the earth and grow a great nation
full of heroic men. No, thank you, sir. Yes,
you may take my picture. No, I'm not Cinderella.
I never liked fairy tales because I don't like the myth
of the charming man. But the witchy woman,
she's real. I drink hard, I smoke hard, I do everything
to excess and it will make a man's clothes melt
right off his body. What do I say to those who laugh
at me, sir? You have every right to laugh, so long
as you can laugh at yourself first. Yes, I'm really sure
I don't want marriage—I didn't do this for the apron
and the poodle skirt. Look, I don't need
a husband; I don't need to bargain
to get what I want. I know what you're going to write
about me: you're going to say I tossed off my Bloody Mary
like a guy. You're going to marvel at my hip-swinging
gait, my slim, trembling fingers, my girlish giggle,
my rosy blush. Not girl enough in one sentence.
Perplexingly girl in the next. I don't care. I can tell
you how to find paradise but you'll never write
it down: be who you are, don't be too bizarre,
expect very little from this world,
and don't be surprised when a woman
gives a revolution a swift kick in the ass.

Christine Jorgensen was the first American trans woman to become widely known for having sex reassignment surgery. Jorgensen served in the army during WWII, and her surgery attracted a significant amount of press. She worked as an actress, singer, and nightclub entertainer, and she was known for her bluntness and intelligent wit. Some sentiments in the poem come from her interviews.

Desaparecida / Disappeared

Carol Dine

—*Susana Trimarco, Argentina*

In the brothel,
I ask the girls:
have you seen
two men, a gun
a red car with tinted windows
my Marita.

They're waiting in a line
against the wall;
their black nylons
have crooked seams.

I hold up the photograph;
my daughter, grinning,
models her new plaid mini skirt,
the high, shiny boots.

Can the dead walk?
Can the disappeared touch
my skin
for an instant,
like an eyelash
come loose?

*Susana Trimarco's daughter, Marita, was kidnapped in 2002 and never found.
A human rights activist, Trimarco works to combat human trafficking.*

Rana Plaza: Shaheena

Nancy Clarke Otter

I woke up in my grave before I died.
Not once, but time and darkening time again.
I'd heard the floor explode and then the space
that was the room changed places with the wall.
I was drowned in brick, was gripped, was turned
to dust, became a mote of broken plaster,
became the blinded space within the crack,
a gritted tongue of gravel filled my mouth.
I moaned—a kind of ecstasy this death.

But I was not so dead I couldn't hear.
I heard the fire fighters' calling, and
their weeping. They said *We came for you*
before we knew your name. But oh, we lost you
to the sour greed of flame.

In April 2013, Rana Plaza, a clothing factory building in Bangladesh supplying
several US retailers, collapsed with more than 3,000 workers inside. A woman
named Shaheena survived seven days trapped in the rubble, but died in fire
that swept through the tunnel dug by rescue workers trying to reach her.

The Mines of South Africa

Alice Pettway

are swallowing the men
of Mozambique in gulps
down gullets grimed with coal dust
and reeking of false opportunity.
Stories of money and sex
unroll, a great tongue
lapping up boys too young
to recognize the danger
and men too old to resist
the temptation of success
after so many years of failure.

The women of one country
take in the men of the women
stranded in the other,
give their bodies like stone
to be cracked open and stripped
until they are chiseled
clean of their ore.

The men grow tired
and slow, and the mines vomit
the men of Mozambique,
heaving them slick with sweat
and swollen with disease
back to their families.

And the women in one country
take in the men who have had
the women in the other,
give their bodies like water
to cool the heat of shame
until they are desiccated
by their husbands' illnesses.

The mines of South Africa
are swallowing
the women of Mozambique.

Sonora Desert

Renny Golden

for Josseline Jamileth Hernández Quinteros

Josseline still stands there in his mind
sun glare washing her black hair

to whiteness. The boy
has held her hand for 1500 miles.

He shades his eyes, sees her
becoming the color of the desert.

He tries to free his hand, run back to her
but she calls, *No, go on with them.*

Find Mamá. I'll be all right.
This decision, what love asks

of a fourteen-year-old too weak to walk.
Her farewell wave a surrender

of the world. What she gives is
more than a child's gesture.

On this road she did the one thing
that was hers to do, even as she lies

down now near thorn scrub.
Harris hawks plunge across twilight's

scarlet and plum silence. On the ridge
above the wash, saguaro is sentinel.

She has vomited again and again.
Mamá, Mamá. Scorpions and jackrabbits,

everything luminous in moonrise.
Cold rising, faint last birdsong.

Her head on a rock pillow
until her shivering ceases, ceases.

By February they'll find her beaded bracelet,
green sneakers, her bones. The Tumacácori wilderness

hisses. Spanish soldiers called it—*The Emptiness.*

Josseline died in the desert in 2008. She was 14. Her brother made it to his mother in California. Author Margaret Ragan told her story in The Death of Josseline, Boston: Beacon Press, 2010. According to the Border Patrol 2,701 migrants died in the Sonora desert between 1998 and 2013. In spite of the risks, people continue to cross. As a member of the Albuquerque Faith Coalition on Immigrant justice I interviewed apprehended mothers and children in Artesia Family Detention Center along the New Mexico/Mexico border and also mothers and children in Karnes Family Detention Center in Texas. I never spoke with a mother fleeing gang extortion/beatings/rape in Honduras, El Salvador or Guatemala, that was not in trauma. This story of refugee mothers and children is hidden.

An Almost Impossible Friendship

Natalie Lobe

The Washington Post, July 13, 2014

Not far from the border at Gaza lies an indifferent sea,
tide brushing war-torn shores, sand riddled with alien shells.

From opposite sides of the border, a friendship thrives
like a marsh rose in the desert. Maha, the Arab
and Roni, the Jew, phone and text all day. *Are you coping?*

Roni works a farm 800 yards from the border.
Maha, a translator, shares a flat in Gaza City.
They met when Maha crossed over for medical help.
No one crosses now, except soldiers with grenades.
Their countrymen sneer, *Friends?*
The women persevere. Sometimes they are afraid.

Their dream is to sip tea together in the quiet
of an afternoon, watch the children play on the beach,
laugh about the foibles of an ordinary day.

Today, it is the blip of a cell phone and thin voices
barely heard above the sirens and screaming—
Take care, my friend. Take care.

Happy Is How I'll Look

Weathering

Fleur Adcock

Literally thin-skinned, I suppose, my face catches the wind
off the snow-line and flushes
with a flush that will never wholly settle. Well:
that was a metropolitan vanity,
wanting to look young forever, to pass.

I was never a pre-Raphaelite beauty
and only pretty enough to satisfy
men who need to be seen with a passable woman.
But now that I am in love with a place
which doesn't care how I look, or if I'm happy,

happy is how I look and that's all.
My hair will grow gray in any case,
my nails chip and flake, my waist thicken,
and the years will work all their usual changes.
If my face is to be weather beaten as well,

that's little enough lost, a fair bargain
for a year among the lakes and vales, when simply
to look out of my window at the high pass
makes me indifferent to mirrors and to what
my soul may wear over its new complexion.

Notes on the Contributors

Fleur Adcock was born in Auckland, New Zealand, and has also spent many years in England. She has earned many honors including the New Zealand National Book Award, the Cholmondeley Award, and the Queen's Gold Medal for Poetry. Adcock is the author of over ten poetry collections and the editor of three poetry collections.

Laura Altshul's first collection of poetry, *Searching for the Northern Lights*, was published in the summer of 2015. She was the featured poet on the public TV series *Speaking of Poetry Episode 36*. She lives in New Haven, Connecticut.

Joseph Bathanti is the author of 17 books and is the former poet laureate of North Carolina. He teaches at Appalachian State University in Boone, North Carolina.

Christine Beck holds a Master of Fine Arts in Creative Writing degree from Southern Connecticut State University and is the author of *Blinding Light* (Grayson Books 2013), *I'm Dating Myself*, (Dancing Girl Press 2015), and *Stirred, Not Shaken* (Five Oaks Press 2016). She is the Poet Laureate of West Hartford, Connecticut (2015-17). She has been an active board member of The Connecticut Poetry Society since 2006. More information about her many activities is on her website: www.ChristineBeck.net.

Sherri (Sheryll) Bedingfield's poetry has been published in numerous anthologies and small press publications, including *Connecticut River Review, Caduceus*, and *Journal of Poetry Therapy*. She's presented her poetry in Dingle, Ireland and many other venues, including Word Forge Reading Series in Hartford, the Noah Webster House in West Hartford, the Yale Book Store, and New York City's Cornelia Street Café. She is the author of two poetry collections *Transitions and Transformations* (Antrim House, 2010) and *The Clattering* (Grayson Books, 2016). Bedingfield works as a psychotherapist and family therapist.

Carol Berg's poems are forthcoming or in *DMQ Review, Sou'wester, The Journal, Spillway, Redactions, Radar Poetry, Verse Wisconsin*, and elsewhere. Her chapbook, *Her Vena Amoris* (Red Bird Chapbooks), is available and her chapbooks, *Ophelia Unraveling* and *The Ornithologist Poems*, are both available from dancing girl press. She was a recipient of a finalist grant from the Massachusetts Cultural Council.

Sue D. Burton is a physician assistant specializing in women's health care. Her poetry has appeared in *Beloit Poetry Journal, Blackbird, Green Mountains Review, Hayden's Ferry Review, New Ohio Review, Shenandoah*, and on *Verse Daily*. Her long poem *Little Steel* has been published as an e-chapbook by *Mudlark*.

Christine Casson is the author of *After the First World*, a book of poems. Her work has appeared in numerous journals and anthologies, and she has also published critical essays on the work of Leslie Marmon Silko and the poetry of Linda Hogan and Robert Penn Warren. She is Scholar-/Writer-in-Residence at Emerson College.

Anne Champion is the author of *Reluctant Mistress and The Dark Length Home*. Her poetry has appeared in *Prairie Schooner, New South, Verse Daily, The Pinch, Redivider*, and elsewhere. She was a Pushcart Prize nominee, a Best of the Net winner, and an Academy of American Poet's Prize recipient. She currently teaches writing in Boston, Massachusetts.

Renny Christopher is Vice Chancellor for Academic Affairs at Washington State University Vancouver. Before earning her doctorate, Christopher worked as a printing press operator, typesetter, carpenter and horse wrangler. Her memoir, *A Carpenter's Daughter: A Working-Class Woman in Higher Education* (Sense Publishers, 2009), addresses her experiences as the first in her family to attend college.

Ann Clark teaches English at SUNY Jefferson in Watertown, NY. Her poems have recently appeared in *Storm Cellar, Poetry Quarterly, The Paterson Literary Review*, and *Rattle*, and her first collection, *No Witness*, has been published by Jane's Boy Books.

Elayne Clift is a writer/journalist, writing workshop leader, and lecturer who has also worked and taught internationally with a focus on women and gender and maternal/child health. Her journalism, fiction, poetry and creative nonfiction have appeared in various publications and anthologies internationally. In 2012 she published her novel, *Hester's Daughters*, based on *The Scarlet Letter,* and in 2014 her third short story collection, *Children of the Chalet*, won First Prize/Fiction from Greyden Press, which published it in 2015. (www.elayne-clift.com)

Mark DeFoe teaches in WV Wesleyan's MFA in Writing program. He has published ten books of poetry. He lives in Buckhannon, West Virginia with his wife Jeanne, a pianist.

Carol Dine's most recent book, *Orange Night*, features her poems accompanied by images of artist and Holocaust survivor Samuel Bak. Her previous book, *Van Gogh in Poems*, written as if in the artist's voice, includes 18 images of Van Gogh's drawings. Dine's memoir, *Places in the Bone*, deals with the redemptive power of writing. She teaches poetry and memoir at Massachusetts College of Art & Design.

Lisa Dordal (M.Div., M.F.A.) teaches in the English Department at Vanderbilt University. A Pushcart Prize nominee and the recipient of an Academy of American Poets Prize, her poetry has appeared in a variety of journals including *Best New Poets, CALYX, The Greensboro Review, Vinyl Poetry*, and *The Journal of Feminist Studies in Religion*. Her first full-length collection of poetry, *Mosaic of the Dark*, is forthcoming from Black Lawrence Press.

Rita Dove is a former U.S. Poet Laureate (1993-1995) and recipient of the 1987 Pulitzer Prize in poetry for *Thomas and Beulah*. The author of ten poetry collections, most recently *Collected Poems 1974-2004* (2016) and *Sonata Mulattica* (2009), as well as a collection of short stories, a novel, a play and a song cycle (with composer John Williams), she also edited *The Penguin Anthology of Twentieth-Century American Poetry* (2011). She has received numerous honors, among them the 1996 National Humanities Medal from President Clinton and the 2011 National Medal of Arts from President Obama. Rita Dove is Commonwealth Professor of English at the University of Virginia.

Juditha Dowd has authored three chapbooks and a full-length collection. Her poems have appeared in *Florida Review, Spillway, Ekphrasis, Canary, Cider Press Review* and elsewhere. She's a member of the ensemble Cool Women performing in the NY-Philadelphia metro region. *Dearest Eliza* is part of a verse narrative, "Audubon's Sparrow," that follows the couple's life on the frontier and later in New Orleans.

Jacqueline Doyle has published, in addition to scholarly articles, creative work in literary journals such as *Southern Humanities Review, Quarter After Eight, [PANK], Confrontation, The Pinch, Southern Indiana Review*, and *Catamaran Literary Reader*. Her work has earned Notable Essay citations in Best American Essays 2013 and Best American Essays 2015, two Pushcart nominations, a Best of the Net nomination, and numerous prizes. She teaches at California State University, East Bay.

Tina Egnoski is the author of *In the Time of the Feast of Flowers*, winner of the 2010 Clay Reynolds Novella Prize, and the chapbook *Perishables*. Her work, both poetry and fiction, has been published in a number of literary journals, including *The Carolina Quarterly, Cimarron Review, The Masters Review* and *Saw Palm Journal*. She's the director of the Ocean State Summer Writing Conference.

Susan Erickson's collection of poems, *Lauren Bacall Shares a Limousine*, won the Brick Road Poetry Prize and will be published in 2017. The poems are in the voices of women, both famous and forgotten. Erickson lives in Bellingham, Washington, where she helped establish the Sue C. Boynton Poetry Walk and Contest.

Maureen Tolman Flannery is the author of eight books of poetry, including *Tunnel into Morning, Destiny Whispers to the Beloved*, and *Ancestors in the Landscape*. She is a Wyoming sheep rancher's daughter who now lives in Chicago, where she is an English teacher, wood carver and Home Funeral Guide. More than five hundred of her poems have been published in anthologies, journals and literary reviews.

CB Follett has eleven books of poetry, plus several chapbooks. Her poems have been nominated for nine Pushcart Prizes, and she has been nominated ten times as an individual poet. Widely published and awarded, she is Poet Laureate Emerita of Marin County. (2010-2013).

Jennifer L. Freed's poems have appeared in various literary magazines including *Poetry East, Atlanta Review, Cloudbank, and Common Ground Review*, in the medical journals *JAMA* and *Chest*, and in a chapbook, *These Hands Still Holding*, a finalist for the 2013 New Women's Voices chapbook contest. She lives with her husband and children in Massachusetts.

Carol Frith, co-editor of *Ekphrasis*, has chapbooks from *Gribble Press, Palanquin Press*, and *Finishing Line*, among others. Her latest book is from *FutureCycle Press*. Frith's work has appeared in *Seattle Review, Midwest Quarterly, Rattle, RHINO, Smartish Pace, Measure, The Formalist* and elsewhere.

Carmen Germain is the author of *These Things I Will Take with Me* (Cherry Grove). Recent work has appeared in *Poet Lore, Fifth Wednesday*, and *Harpur Palate*. Also a surface design and visual artist, she lives in Washington state.

Maria Mazziotti Gillan, the author of twenty-one books, received the American Book Award for *All That Lies Between Us* (Guernica Editions). Among her other awards is the 2014 George Garrett Award for Outstanding Community Service in Literature from AWP (Association of Writers and Writing Programs). Ms. Gillan is the Founder and Executive Director of the Poetry Center at Passaic County Community College in Paterson, New Jersey and editor of the Paterson Literary Review. She is also Director of the Creative Writing Program and Professor of Poetry at Binghamton University-SUNY.

Renny Golden's *Blood Desert: Witnesses 1820-1880,* University of New Mexico Press, won the WILLA Literary Award for poetry 2011, was named a Southwest Notable Book of the Year 2012 and a Finalist for the New Mexico Book Award. Golden has been published in *Water~Stone, International Quarterly, Literary Review, Dogwood, Main Street Rag, and Borderlands: Texas Poetry Review.* Her work is anthologized in *Irish American Poetry* (Notre Dame Press). She earned a Pushcart nomination in 2016.

Judy Grahn's poem *Ella in a square apron, along Highway 80* has been forgotten by the elitist economy for twenty years; hopefully a new generation will take up her cause. Judy Grahn wrote "Ella" as one of seven "Common Woman Poems" in 1969, and they helped fuel the feminist movement. Ms. Grahn has since published 14 books, won many awards, been Grand Marshall of two Gay Pride parades, has a nonfiction award named for her, and continues to teach, travel, and perform her complex work.

Bridget Grieve-Carlson is a special education aide in an elementary classroom. Her short stories have been published in *The Storyteller, Central PA Magazine* and *Roanoke Review.* In addition, she has just completed her first novel.

Pat Hale's poetry collection, *Seeing Them with My Eyes Closed,* was published in 2015 by Grayson Books. She has been awarded CALYX's Lois Cranston Memorial Poetry Prize, the Sunken Garden Poetry Prize, and first prize in the Al Savard Poetry Competition. In 2011, the Hill-Stead Museum published her chapbook, *Composition and Flight.* She serves on the board of directors for the Riverwood Poetry Series.

Vernita Hall finished second in *American Literary Review*'s Creative Nonfiction Contest; was a finalist for: Cutthroat's Barry Lopez Nonfiction, Rita Dove Poetry, and Paumanok Poetry Awards; and a *Naugatuck River Review* Narrative Poetry Contest semi-finalist. Chapbook *The Hitchhiking Robot Learns About Philadelphians* won the 2016 Moonstone Chapbook Contest. Poems and essays have appeared/are forthcoming in *Atlanta Review*, *Philadelphia Stories*, *Referential*, *MezzoCammin*, *Whirlwind*, *Canary*, *African American Review*, and six anthologies.

Lenore Hart also writes as Elisabeth Graves. She's the author of nine books, including *Waterwoman*, a B & N Discover Award novel. She's received awards and fellowships for fiction, nonfiction, and poetry, and has been featured in *Poets and Writers*, on *Voices of America*, and PBS's *Writer to Writer*. Two novels are optioned for film. Hart teaches at The Mailer Center, Ossabaw Island Retreat, and in Wilkes University's MFA writing program.

Grey Held has spent 25 years in the corporate world, managing and mentoring teams and coordinating projects. He is a recipient of an NEA Fellowship in Creative Writing. Two books of his poetry have been published: *Two-Star General* (Brick Road Poetry Press in 2012) and *Spilled Milk* (Word Press in 2013). Held works closely with the Mayor's Office of Cultural Affairs in Newton, Massachusetts to direct projects that connect contemporary poets (and their poetry) with a wider audience.

Elise Hempel's poems have appeared in many journals, including *Poetry*, *The Midwest Quarterly*, *Valparaiso Poetry Review*, *Measure, and The Evansville Review*, as well as in Ted Kooser's *American Life in Poetry*. Her first full-length collection of poems, *Second Rain*, is available from Able Muse Press.

Joan Hofmann is professor emeritus at the University of Saint Joseph in West Hartford, Connecticut. Her poetry has been published in journals and anthologized in books. She serves on the Boards of the Riverwood Poetry and the Connecticut Poetry Society, is a member of the Connecticut Coalition of Poets Laureate, and is the Poet Laureate of Canton, Connecticut. In 2014, Antrim House Books published her collection of poetry, *Coming Back*.

Jodi Hottel's work has been published in *Nimrod International*, *Spillway*, *Naugatuck Review*, *Touch* and anthologies from the University of Iowa Press and Tebot Bach. *Heart Mountain*, her chapbook of poems about the Japanese American incarceration, was winner of the 2012 Blue Light Press Poetry Prize.

Tony Howarth, a playwright and former journalist, retired in 1991 after 28 years as a high school teacher of English and theatre. Much of his poetry focuses on the idylls and trauma of being old.

H.K. Hummel is an assistant professor of creative writing at the University of Arkansas at Little Rock. She is the author of the chapbooks *Boytreebird* (Finishing Line Press, 2013) and *Handmade Boats* (Whale Sound, 2010), and co-author of the textbook *Short-form Creative Writing: A Writer's Guide and Anthology* (Bloomsbury, 2018). Her poems have recently appeared in *Flyway: Journal of Writing & Environment*, *Meridian*, *Booth*, and *Iron Horse Review*.

Esther Whitman Johnson, a former high school educator, travels the globe as a volunteer, often writing about her journeys. Among the venues in which her work has appeared or is forthcoming are *Artemis*, *Broad River Review*, *Dirty Chai*, *Earth's Daughters*, *eno*, *Lunch Ticket*, *Main St. Rag*, *The Well-Versed Reader*, and *Virginia Writers*.

Janet Joyner's prize-winning poems have been honored by The South Carolina Poetry Society and the North Carolina Poetry Council, as well as anthologized in *The Southern Poetry Anthology, volume vii: North Carolina*, and *Second Spring 2016*. Her first collection of poems, *Waterborne*, the 2015 winner of the Holland Prize, was published in February, 2016, by Logan House.

Marilyn Kallet, who wrote the introduction for this collection, is Nancy Moore Goslee Professor of English, University of Tennessee; poet and author of 17 books, including *Sleeping With One Eye Open: Women Writers and the Art of Survival*, University of Georgia Press, co-edited with Judith Ortiz Cofer; *Worlds in Our Words: Contemporary American Women Writers*, Prentice Hall, co-edited with Patricia Clark; *The Moveable Nest: A Mother-Daughter Companion*, Helicon Nine; *A House of Gathering: Poets on May Sarton's Poetry*, University of Tennessee Press. Dr. Kallet also leads a poetry workshop every year in Auvillar, France, as part of the VCCA-France program.

Catherine Keefe is a California poet, essayist, and the founding editor of dirtcakes, a journal inspired by the UN Millennial Goals to eradicate poverty. Recent creative nonfiction and poetry appear, or are forthcoming, in *Cactus Heart, Gettysburg Review, Sugar House Review, TAB: The Journal of Poetry & Poetics*, and *Zócalo Public Square.*

Nancy Kerrigan has worked as a psychotherapist in private & public hospitals, community mental health settings and in independent practice. Kerrigan is an alumnus of Wesleyan University's Writers Week and workshops at the Frost Place in Franconia, New Hampshire. Her poetry appears in numerous journals and anthologies. She is the author of the chapbook, *The Voices: The Poetry of Psychiatry* (Finishing Line Press, 2009).

Janet R. Kirchheimer is the author of *How to Spot One of Us*, (2007). Currently, she is producing *AFTER*, a cinematic documentary showcasing poetry about the Holocaust. Her work has appeared in journals including *Atlanta Review, Limestone, Connecticut Review, Natural Bridge* and on forward.com and collegevilleinstitute.com. She is a Pushcart Prize nominee and received a Drisha Institute for Jewish Education Arts Fellowship.

Ted Kooser is the author of thirteen poetry collections and numerous nonfiction books, children's books, and chapbooks. He has received dozens of awards and served two terms as the Poet Laureate of the United States. He edits a weekly newspaper column, "American Life in Poetry," which reaches a worldwide audience, in print and online, of 3.5 million readers. He is a Presidential Professor at the University of Nebraska, where he teaches the writing of poetry.

Charlene Langfur is a Southern Californian, an organic gardener, and a Syracuse University Graduate Writing Fellow. Her poems and essays have appeared in many magazines and journals; most recently a series of poems was featured in *Poetry East.*

Natalie Lobe's chapbook, *Conversation with Abraham* was published in May, 2012, *Connected Voices* was published in 2006 and *Island Time* in 2008. Her poems have appeared in *Slant, Jewish Currents, Comstock Review, California Quarterly*, and others. As a poet in the schools, Natalie has taught in dozens of elementary schools as well as in Anne Arundel Community College. She reviewed poetry for the *Montserrat Review* 2008-2011. Her fourth collection of poems is ready for publication.

Mary Makofske's book, *Traction* (Ashland Poetry, 2011) won the Richard Snyder Prize. Her other books are *The Disappearance of Gargolyles* and *Eating Nasturiums*, winner of a Flume Press chapbook competition. Her poems have appeared in *Southern Poetry Review*, *Poetry East*, *Asheville Poetry Review*, *Poetry Daily*, *Calyx*, and other journals, as well as in fourteen anthologies. She received 2nd place in the 2015 Allen Ginsberg Awards. Makofske lives in Warwick, NY.

Paul Martin's book *Closing Distances* was published by The Backwaters Press. He is also the author of two prize-winning chapbooks: *Floating on the Lehigh* (Grayson Books) and *Rooms of the Living* (Autumn House Press).

Kathleen McClung, author of *Almost the Rowboat*, has poems in *Mezzo Cammin*, *Ekphrasis*, *Heron Tree*, *Naugatuck River Review*, *Raising Lilly Ledbetter: Women Poets Occupy the Workspace*, and elsewhere. Winner of the Rita Dove Poetry Prize and Ina Coolbrith Circle awards, she judges sonnets for the Soul-Making Keats literary competition and teaches at Skyline College and the Writing Salon. She lives in San Francisco. Learn more at: www.kathleenmcclung.com.

Karla Linn Merrifield is a nine-time Pushcart-Prize nominee and National Park Artist-in-Residence. Merrifield has had over 500 poems appear in dozens of journals and anthologies. She has twelve books to her credit; the newest is *Bunchberries, More Poems of Canada*, a sequel to the award-winning *Godwit: Poems of Canada* (FootHills). She is assistant editor/poetry book reviewer for *The Centrifugal Eye*. Visit her blog, Vagabond Poet, at: http://karlalinn.blogspot.com.

Ilene Millman is a speech/language pathologist currently working with preschool children and volunteering as tutor and tutor trainer for Literacy Volunteers in New Jersey. Her poems have appeared in a variety of literary journals including *The Sow's Ear*, *Paterson Literary Review*, *Adanna*, *Poetica*, and *US1 Worksheets*. She won honorable mention in the 2016 Anna Davidson Rosenberg Poetry Contest.

Eileen Moeller lives in the Philadelphia area. She's had poems in *Ars Medica*, *Feminist Studies*, *Paterson Literary Review*, *Blue Fifth Review*, *Schuylkill Valley Journal*, *Philadelphia Stories*, and in several anthologies. Her book: *Firefly, Brightly Burning*, is available from Grayson Books, and a chapbook, *The Girls In Their Iron Shoes*, is from Finishing Line Press. Access her blog: And So I Sing: Poems And Iconography, online.

Pat Mottola is an award-winning poet and Pushcart Prize nominee currently teaching creative writing at Southern Connecticut State University. In addition to working with students at S.C.S.U., she is thrilled to teach both art and poetry to senior citizens throughout Connecticut. Pat is the co-editor of *Connecticut River Review* and the author of *Under the Red Dress* (Five Oaks Press). She is most proud of her latest endeavor – mentoring Afghan women through the Afghan Women's Writing Project.

Sheila Murphy, a retired teacher, edited *Fair Warning: Leo Connellan and His Poetry* (2011). Her chapbook, *View from a Kayak in Autumn* (2008), honors the memory of two grandchildren who died of Spinal Muscular Atrophy. She directs memoir and poetry workshops at the Wesleyan Institute for Lifelong Learning. She and her husband live in Connecticut with their Welsh corgi.

Carol Nolde's poetry was anthologized in *Knowing Stones: Poems of Exotic Places*, the second edition of *Love is Ageless: Stories about Alzheimer's Disease, Child of my Child*, and *Richer Resources*. Her chapbook *Comfort in Stone* was published by Finishing Line Press in 2014. She and her family live in Westfield, New Jersey, where she taught English and creative writing and for many years was an associate editor for *Merlyn's Pen*, a national magazine devoted to the work of teenage writers.

Renée Olander was born on the Naval Base in Corpus Christie, Texas and grew up on and around military bases in California, Michigan, Hawai'i, and Virginia. Her poems have appeared in journals and in *A Few Spells* (Finishing Line Press, 2010). She received the Kate Smith Award for Poetry (*Amelia Magazine*) and a Pushcart Prize nomination (*Sistersong: Women Across Cultures*).

Nancy Clarke Otter is a poet and essayist, and teaches English at a public school in Hartford, Connecticut. Her poems have appeared in the *Wallace Stevens Journal, Naugatuck River Review, Blue Collar Review, Earth's Daughters, Ekphrasis*, and *CALYX*. In 2014 her poem, "Fortune's Rest," won the Connecticut Poetry Award. She recently completed an MFA in creative writing at Goddard College.

Sheila Packa lives in northern Minnesota and writes essays, stories and poems. She teaches creative writing and has four books of poems. She was the 2010-2012 Duluth Poet Laureate. See her blog at: www.sheilapacka.com.

Julia Paul's poems are published in numerous journals and anthologies, both national and international, and several of her poems have been performed in stage productions. Her first book, *Shook*, was published by Grayson Books. She is an elder law attorney in Manchester, Connecticut. Since 2014, Paul has served as Manchester, Connecticut's first Poet Laureate.

Alice Pettway's work has appeared in a variety of print and online journals, including *The Bitter Oleander*, *The Connecticut Review*, *Folio*, and *WomenArts Quarterly*. Her first full-length collection, *The Time of Hunger*, is forthcoming from Salmon Poetry in 2017. Pettway is a former Lily Peter fellow, Raymond L. Barnes Poetry Award winner, and three-time Pushcart Prize nominee. Currently, she lives and writes in Bogotá, Colombia.

Teresa Poore has lived and been inspired to write poetry on the east coast, gulf coast, and now the west coast. She is a practicing psychotherapist, in the San Francisco Bay Area. Her poetry has appeared in publications such as *Old Red Kimono* and *Red Rock Review*. Ms. Poore won first prize in the poetry category of the 2015 Soul-Making Keats Literary Competition.

Elena Lelia Radulescu's poetry, short stories, and essays have appeared in *Vision International*, *Into the Teeth of the Wind*, *Square Lake Review*, *The Spoon River Poetry Review*, *Chelsea*, *Karamu*, *CALXY*, *Mutabilis Press Anthology of Poetry*, *Texas Poetry Calendar*, *Magnolia Journal*, *Romanian Literary Review*, and other publications. In 2014 Radulescu was a finalist in The Southern Women Poetry Contest. She lives in Katy, Texas, where she is working on a novel-in-verse for middle-grade children.

kerry rawlinson gravitated decades ago from sunny Zambian skies to solid Canadian soil. In this second career, following poetry & art's Muses, barefoot, she's has won contests in *Postcard Poems and Prose*, in *Geist Magazine* and placed as a finalist in others. Her writing and her photo-artwork is featured in several lit-mags, including *CanLit*, *Codex*, *ditchpoetry*, *3Elements Review*, *Section8 Magazine*, *Qwerty*; and *Adirondack Review*.

Sherry Rind is the author of four collections of poetry and editor of two books about Airedale terriers. She has received awards from the National Endowment for the Arts, Anhinga Press, Artist Trust, Seattle Arts Commission, and King County Arts Commission. She teaches at Lake Washington Institute of Technology.

Cinthia Ritchie writes and runs mountain trails in Anchorage, Alaska, with her dog, Seriously. She's a Pushcart Prize nominee and recipient of a Best American Essay 2013 Notable Mention. Find her work at *Evening Street Review, Under the Sun, Water-Stone Review, damfino Press, Best American Sports Writing 2013, New York Times Magazine, Mary, Third Wednesday, Miller's Pond, Foliate Oak Review, Sport Literate* and others. Her first novel, *Dolls Behaving Badly*, was released from Hachette Book Group. She blogs about writing and Alaska life at: www.cinthiaritchie.com.

Edwin Romond is the author of eight collections of poetry and has been awarded fellowships from the National Endowment for the Arts, as well as from both the New Jersey and Pennsylvania State Councils on the Arts. He is the recipient of the 2013 New Jersey Poetry Prize for his poem, "Champion."

Lynn Veach Sadler, a former college president, has published five books and 72 articles, edited 22 books/proceedings and three national journals, and writes two newspaper columns. Her creative writing publications are ten poetry chapbooks (another forthcoming) and four full-length collections, over a hundred short stories, 41 plays, four novels, a novella, a fiction collection (with two more forthcoming), and a nonfiction collection (forthcoming). She was a Gilbert-Chappell Distinguished Poet (2013-2015).

Rikki Santer's work has appeared in numerous publications, including *Ms. Magazine, Poetry East, Margie, Crab Orchard Review, Grimm*, and *The Main Street Rag*. Her fifth and newest collection, *The Syntax of Trouble*, is forthcoming from NightBallet Press. She lives in Columbus, Ohio, where she teaches literature, writing, and film studies at a public high school. Learn more at: www.rikkisanter.com.

Lynn Schmeidler's poems have appeared in numerous literary magazines including *Barrow Street, Boston Review*, and *Fence*, as well as various anthologies including *Drawn to Marvel: Poems from the Comic Books* (Minor Arcana Press), *Mischief, Caprice and Other Poetic Strategies* (Red Hen Press), *Out of Sequence: The Sonnets Remixed* (Parlor Press), and *Bared* (Les Femmes Folles Books). Her chapbook, *Curiouser & Curiouser* was published by Grayson Books.

Heather Schroeder is a poet, fiction writer, and essayist who lives in Knoxville, Tennessee. Her nonfiction book *A Reader's Guide to Marjane Satrapi's 'Persepolis'* was released by Enslow Publishing, and her fiction, poetry and essays have appeared in *Southern Indiana Review, bornmagazine. com, Iron Horse Literary Review, Wisconsin People and Ideas, Beloit Fiction Journal, The Virginia Quarterly Review*, and *The Cream City Review*.

Paula Sergi is a Wisconsin writer with an interest in all things mid-century, including memories. She's published three poetry chapbooks and edited three anthologies.

Pegi Deitz Shea has published more than 400 works of fiction, nonfiction, poetry, and children's books. She teaches in the Creative Writing programs at the University of Connecticut, the Mark Twain House in Hartford, and the Institute for Writers.

Vivian Shipley published two books of poetry in 2015, *Perennial* (Negative Capability Press, Mobile, AL), and *The Poet* (Louisisana Literature Press, SLU, Hammond, LA). Shipley's ninth book, *All of Your Messages Have Been Erased* (Louisiana Literature Press, 2010) won the Sheila Motton Book Prize from the New England Poetry Club, the Paterson Award for Sustained Literary Achievement, and the CT Press Club Award for Best Creative Writing. She has received the Paterson Literary Review Award for Lifetime Service to Literature, the Library of Congress's Connecticut Lifetime Achievement Award for Service to the Literary Community, and the Connecticut Book Award for Poetry two times.

Maxine Susman lives in central New Jersey. She writes about nature, art, and personal history, and has published six chapbooks, most recently *Provincelands* (2016) set on Cape Cod. Her poems appear in *Fourth River, Poet Lore, Blueline, Journal of New Jersey Poets, Paterson Literary Review, Adanna*, and elsewhere. She teaches poetry writing and short stories through the Osher Lifelong Learning Institute of Rutgers University.

Susan Terris' recent books are *Ghost of Yesterday: New & Selected Poems* (Marsh Hawk Press) and *Memos* (Omnidawn). Journal publications include *Denver Quarterly, Field*, and *Ploughshares*. A poem from *Field* appeared in Pushcart Prize XXXI. A poem from Memos is in *Best American Poetry* 2015. She's editor of *Spillway Magazine*. Visit: http://www.susanterris.com.

Mary Langer Thompson's poems, short stories, and essays appear in various journals and anthologies, most recently *Altadena Poetry Review*. She is a contributor to two poetry writing texts, *The Working Poet* (Autumn Press, 2009) and *Women and Poetry: Writing, Revising, Publishing and Teaching* (McFarland, 2012). A retired school principal and former secondary English teacher, Langer Thompson received her Ed.D. from the University of California, Los Angeles.

Allison Thorpe is a writer from Lexington, KY. The author of several books of poetry, she has recent work in *So To Speak*, *Crab Fat*, *Green Hills Literary Lantern*, *Poetry Pacific*, *Still: The Journal*, *The Homestead Review*, *Gingerbread House*, *Muddy River Poetry Review*, and *Yellow Chair Review*.

Psyche North Torok was raised among bumpkins in rural northeast Ohio. She is a graduate of Ohio State University. Her poetry reflects the spiritual and sensual qualities inherent in all life, visible, she believes, to any who have the passion to seek them. She lives in Columbus, Ohio.

Karen Torop is a poet and psychotherapist in Middletown, Connecticut. Her poems have appeared in *Alligator Juniper*, *Atlanta Review*, *Connecticut Review*, *Connecticut River Review*, *Emily Dickinson Award Anthology* (Universities West Press), *The Ledge*, and *Theodate*.

Alison Townsend won the 2016 Jeanne Leiby Prose Chapbook Award for *The Persistence of Rivers: An Essay on Moving Water*. She is also the author of two award-winning books of poetry: *The Blue Dress* and *Persephone in America*, and two chapbooks: *And Still the Music*, and *What the Body Knows*. Her work appears widely, and she has received many awards, including a Pushcart Prize, publication in Best American Poetry, a literary arts fellowship from the Wisconsin Arts Board, and the University of Wisconsin-Whitewater's Chancellor's Regional Literary. She is Emerita Professor of English at the University of Wisconsin-Whitewater and lives in the farm country outside Madison.

Memye Curtis Tucker is the author of *The Watchers* (Hollis Summers Poetry Prize, Ohio University Press), three prizewinning chapbooks, and poems appearing in *Poetry Daily*, various journals, and anthologies. With fellowships from MacDowell, VCCA, and Georgia Council for the Arts, a "must read" citation from the Georgia Center for the Book, and a Ph.D. in English literature, she teaches advanced poetry writing and is a Senior Editor at Atlanta Review.

Denise Utt is a poet living in New York City. Her work has appeared in *The Bryant Literary Review, Confrontation, The Evansville Review*, and other journals. She also wrote the lyrics to the song "What I Wouldn't Do (for the Love of You)."

DianaLee Velie lives and writes in Newbury, New Hampshire. She has taught poetry, memoir, and short story at universities and colleges in New York, Connecticut and New Hampshire and in private workshops throughout the United States, Canada and Europe. Her award-winning poetry and short stories have been published in hundreds of literary journals and many have been translated into Italian. Her play, *Mama Says*, was directed by Daniel Quinn in a staged reading in New York City. She is the author of five books of poetry: *Glass House, First Edition, The Many Roads to Paradise, The Alchemy of Desire, Ever After* and a collection of short stories, *Soul Proprietorship: Women in Search of Their Souls*.

Tim Vincent, Ph.D., teaches writing and literature at Duquesne University in Pittsburgh, Pennsylvania.

Jeanne Wagner is the winner of the 2014 Sow's Ear Poetry Review Award and the 2015 Arts & Letters Rumi Award, judged by Stephen Dunn. Her poems have appeared in *The Cincinnati Review, Hayden's Ferry, Alaska Quarterly Review, Shenandoah* and *American Life in Poetry*. The author of five collections, her most recent book, *In the Body of Our Lives*, was released by Sixteen Rivers press in 2011. She is on the editorial board of the *California Quarterly*.

Janet Lee Warman, born in Richmond, Virginia, is currently Professor of English and Education at Elon University in North Carolina. She's had poems published in numerous small journals, nationally and internationally. "Paralysis" is part of an unpublished manuscript, *Pas de Deux*, in the voices of women who were mistresses of famous men.

Lillo Way's poems have appeared or are forthcoming in such publications as *Poet Lore, Tampa Review, New Orleans Review, Madison Review, The Sow's Ear Poetry Review, Poetry East, Common Ground Review, Third Wednesday, Yemassee, Santa Fe Literary Review*, and *WomenArts Quarterly*.

Suellen Wedmore, Poet Laureate emerita for the seaside town of Rockport, Massachusetts, has been widely published. Her chapbook *Deployed* won the Grayson Books contest in 2007, her chapbook *On Marriage and Other Parallel Universes* was published by Finishing Line Press, and recently her chapbook *Mind the Light* was published by Quill's Edge Press. A speech and language therapist in the public schools, she retired to focus on writing and in 2004 graduated from New England College with an MA in Poetry.

Anne Harding Woodworth's fifth book is *Unattached Male* (Poetry Salzburg, 2014). She is also the author of four chapbooks. Her work appears in literary journals in print and on line, in the U.S. and abroad. She lives in Washington, D.C., where she is Vice Chair of the Poetry Board at the Folger Shakespeare Library.

Jeff Worley contributed to two previous Grayson Books anthologies— *Essential Love* and *Proposing on the Brooklyn Bridge*. His most recent book is *A Little Luck*, which won the 2012 X.J. Kennedy Poetry Prize from Texas Review Press, and his poems have appeared in over 500 literary magazines. His website, jeff-worley.com, includes more information about him (he says) than anyone should ever have to know. He lives in Lexington, Kentucky.

Elaine Zimmerman is a poet, essayist and child policy leader. Her poems have been published in numerous poetry journals and anthologies. Poetry honors include the William Stafford, Al Savard and Morton and Elsie Prouty Memorial Awards and a Pushcart nomination. She also writes social narrative and children's policy and is the recipient of the Good Housekeeping Award for Women in Government.

Permission Credits

Fleur Adcock: "Weathering" from *Poems 1960-2000* (Bloodaxe Books, 2000) Reproduced with permission of Bloodaxe Books.

Laura Altshul: "Camille Claudet's Waltz in Bronze" and "Montgomery Bus Arrest: March 2, 1955" are printed by permission of the author.

Joseph Bathanti: "Women's Prison" originally appeared in *Shenandoah* and in *Land of Amnesia* by Joseph Bathanti, (Press 53, 2009), Winston-Salem, NC and is reprinted by permission of the author.

Christine Beck: "Honored" is printed by permission of the author.

Sherri Bedingfield: "Lee Krasner, Artist Forgotten" is reprinted by permission of the author.

Carol Berg: "Belly-Ache with Giant Sphinx Moth: Plate #15 by Maria Sibylla Merian" was first published in *Tinderbox Poetry Journal*, Vol. 1, Issue 2 and is reprinted by permission of the author.

Sue D. Burton: "Letter from Antoinette Bope to Her Sister Mabel, May 24, 1902" was first published in *Beloit Poetry Journal*, Vol.64, No 4, Summer 2015, and is reprinted by permission of the author.

Christine Casson: "Programme Music" first appeared in After the Frist World (Star Cloud Press, Scottsdale, 2008) and is reprinted here by permission of the author.

Anne Champion: "Christine Jorgenson Speaks to the Press" and "Nicknames for Wilma Rudolph" are printed here by permission of the author.

Renny Christopher: "The Rope and the Biplane" and "In the French Laundry" are printed here by permission of the author.

Ann Clark: "My Mother Comes Home Crying from G.E." first appeared in *Rattle: Tribute to Feminist Poets*, Spring, 2016 and is reprinted by permission of the author.

Elayne Clift: "Abandoned Wife with Two Sons" first appeared in *Demons Dancing in My Head: Collected Poems* 1985 – 1995 by Elayne Clift, OGN Publications, 1995, and is reprinted by permission of the author.

Mark DeFoe: "Yearbook Photo: Women's Rifle Team, Cornell—1934" first appeared in *Mid-American Review*, Vol. 5, No.1, 1985, and is reprinted by permission of the author.

Carol Dine: "Desaparecida/Disappeared" is printed here by permission of the author.

Lisa Dordal: "For the Cashier at T.R. Wolfe's Toy and Candy" first appeared in *storySouth*, Issue 40: fall, 2015, and is printed here by permission of the author.

Rita Dove: "Daystar", "Sunday Greens", are from *Thomas and Beulah*, Carnegie-Mellon University Press, © 1986 by Rita Dove, and are reprinted by permission of the author.

Juditha Dowd: "Dearest Eliza" first appeared in *Mango in Winter*, Grayson Books, 2013, and is reprinted by permission of the author.

Jacqueline Doyle: "Practicing Self-Reliance" is printed here by permission of the author.

Tina Egnoski: "The Census Taker" is printed here by permission of the author.

Susan J. Erickson: "Nurses of Bataan" and "Monique Braille's Confession" are printed here by permission of the author.

Maureen Tolman Flannery: "First Indication from the Unknown Half Sister" first appeared in *Siblings: Our First Macrocosm* (Wising Up Press, 2015) and is reprinted here by permission of the author.

CB Follett: "Six-Horse Charley Parkhurst" first appeared in *Wind Rose* (Book four of *Boxing the Compass*), Conflux Press, 2014 and is reprinted here by permission of the author.

Jennifer L. Freed: "Lessons," honorable mention in the 2013 Frank O'Hara prize and in the 2014 Gretchen Warren Award, first appeared in *The Worcester Review*, Vol. 34, 2013, and is reprinted here by permission of the author.

Carol Frith: "After *High Noon*, Edward Hopper" is printed here by permission of the author.

Carmen Germain: "The Dinner Table: Camille" is printed here by permission of the author. "Olga Confronts Modernism" first appeared in *Harpur Palate*, and is reprinted here by permission of the author.

Maria Mazziotti Gillan: "At the Factory Where My Mother Worked" first appeared in *What Blooms in Winter*, New York Quarterly Press, 2016, and is reprinted here by permission of the author.

Renny Golden: "Sonora Desert," honorable mention in the 2016 Split This Rock contest, is reprinted by permission of the author.

Judy Grahn: "Ella in a square apron along highway 80" is reprinted by permission of the author.

Bridget Grieve-Carlson: "The Woman in the House" is printed here by permission of the author.

Pat Hale: "In This Photograph Taken in Arizona" fist appeared in *Composition and Flight*, Hill-Stead Museum, Farmington, Connecticut, 2011, and is reprinted here by permission of the author.

Vernita Hall: "Eulogy" is printed here by permission of the author.

Lenore Hart: "Crazy Quilt, 1918" first appeared in *Turnings: Writings on Women's Transformations*, Norfolk: Old Dominion University, 2000, and is reprinted here by permission of the author.

Grey Held: "Back at the Office" is printed here by permission of the author.

Elise Hempel: "Victorian" first appeared in *Snakeskin*, July, 2015, and is reprinted here by permission of the author.

Joan Hofmann: "Worn Skeins" is printed here by permission of the author.

Jodi Hottel: "Sweeping" first appeared in *Heart Mountain*, Blue Light Press, Fairfield, Iowa, 2012, and is reprinted here by permission of the author.

Tony Howarth: "Four in the Morning" is printed here by permission of the author.

H.K. Hummel: "Elizabeth Eckford's Walk toward Central High School" is printed here by permission of the author.

Esther Johnson: "Haunting the Hemingway House" is printed here by permission of the author.

Janet Joyner: "Ocean's Floor" first appeared in *Waterborne*, Logan House, Wayne, Nebraska, 2016, and is reprinted here by permission of the author.

Catherine Keefe: "On the Last Day When No One Was Looking" first appeared in a different version in the *Tupelo Press 30/30 Project*, online, July, 2013 and is reprinted here by permission of the author.

Nancy Kerrigan: "For the Women Who Ride Buses" first appeared in *Kalliope: A Journal of Women's Literature and Art*, Vol. XXIX, #2, 2007, and is reprinted here by permission of the author.

Janet R. Kirchheimer: "The Photograph in My Hand" first appeared in *Kalliope: A Journal of Women's Literature and Art*, Vol. XXVIII, No. 1, 2006, and is reprinted here by permission of the author.

Ted Kooser: "110th Birthday" and "In a Gift Shop" are from *Splitting an Order*. Copyright ©2014 by Ted Kooser. Harrison. Reprinted with the permission of The Permissions Company, Inc. on behalf of Copper Canyon Press, www.coppercanyonpress.org.

Charlene Langfur: "Some of What I Know About Her' first appeared in *The Voices Project* (Denise Powel: editor), September, 2014, and is reprinted here by permission of the author.

Natalie Lobe: "An Almost Impossible Friendship" is printed here by permission of the author.

Mary Makofske: "Matilda Lawrence" is printed here by permission of the author.

Paul Martin: "Aunt Vilma" first appeared in *Big Muddy*, Vol. 13, Issue 1, 2013 and is reprinted here by permission of the author. "Who I Was" first appeared in *Closing Distances*, The Backwaters Press, Omaha, Nebraska, 2009, and is reprinted here by permission of the author.

Kathleen McClung: The poems "Laura Knight, Self-Portrait, 1913" and "Alice Neel, Nude Self-Portrait, 1980" were first published in *Unsplendid*, July 2014 as sonnets 5 and 6 of "Lighter than Her Lace: A Crown of Borrowed Self-Portraits," a finalist for the 2015 Margaret Reid Prize for Traditional Verse. www.unsplendid.com and www.winningwriters.com. They are reprinted here by permission of the author.

Karla Linn Merrifield: "1842 US Army Expedition-58 days, 85 Soldiers, One Native Guide, One Woman" was first published in *Barrier Island Review*, October 2010, and is reprinted here by permission of the author.

Ilene Millman: "No Mas Bebes" first appeared in *Adanna*, July 2016, and is reprinted here by permission of the author.

Eileen Moeller: "Cemetery" was first published in *Images And Impressions: A Laurel Hill Anthology*, October 2013, sponsored by Laurel Hill cemetery and Manayunk Art Center, both in Philadelphia, Pennsylvania. It is reprinted here by permission of the author.

Pat Mottola: "Perfect Woman" is printed here by permission of the author.

Sheila Murphy: "Shadows Behind the Daughters of Edward Darley Boit" first appeared in *View from a Kayak in Autumn*, Argian Press, Oeonta, New York, 2008 and reprinted here by permission of the author.

Carol Nolde: "From Hulda Crooks' Journal" first appeared in *The Sow's Ear*, and is reprinted here by permission of the author.

Renée Olander: "Grace Sherwood, Witch of Pungo, Advanced in Age" first appeared in *A Few Spells*, Finishing Line Press, Georgetown, Kentucky, 2001, and is reprinted here by permission of the author.

Nancy Clarke Otter: "Rana Plaza" was first published in *Blue Collar Review*, 2014. This poem and "Call Our Names" are printed here by permission of the author.

Sheila Packa: "Unknown Woman Miner" first appeared in *Night Train Red Dust: Poems of the Iron Range*, Wildwood River Press, Duluth, Minnesota, 2014, and is reprinted here by permission of the author.

Julia Paul: "The Jar" and "The Lucky Pillow of Annie Edson Taylor" are printed here by permission of the author.

Alice Pettway: "The Mines of South Africa" first appeared in *WomenArts Quarterly Journal*, winter, 2012. "The Swimmer" first appeared in *The Vehicle*, spring, 2015. These poems are reprinted here by permission of the author.

Teresa Poore: "Cherokee, NC 1878" first appeared in *Red Rock Review*, Spring, 2016 and is reprinted here by permission of the author.

kerry rawlinson: "Number 99" is printed here by permission of the author.

Sherry Rind: "Blue Violin" and "Sarah Stone Paints the O'o Bird" are printed here by permission of the author.

Cinthia Ritchie: "How She Lived" first appeared with a different title in *Evening Street Review*, spring, 2013, and is reprinted here by permission of the author.

Edwin Romond: "Everything about Egypt" firs appeared in *Alone With Love Songs*, Grayson Books, West Hartford, Connecticut, 2011. This poem, and "Something Important" is reprinted here by permission of the author.

Lynn Veach Sadler: "Who Would Let a Black Girl Fly?" first appeared in *Women in Aviation*, Pat Eure, editor, Nags Head, North Carolina, 1999 and is reprinted here by permission of the author.

Rikki Santer: "Codifier" first appeared in *My Cruel Invention*, a poetry anthology published by Meerkat Press, Atlanta, 2015, and is printed here by permission of the author.

Lynn Schmeidler: "Of Unforgettable" is printed here by permission of the author.

Heather Schroeder: "Song of the High Scaler's Wife" is printed here by permission of the author.

Paula Sergi: "Power and Light" first appeared in *Bellevue Literary Review*, fall, 2004, and is printed here by permission of the author. "Sherpa" is printed here by permission of the author.

Pegi Deitz Shea: "Dear Tante Yvette" is printed here by permission of the author.

Vivian Shipley: "May 17, 1720: Superiour Court Justice Counsels Elizabeth Atwood in his Chambers Before Sentencing Her to Hang" and "The Radium Girls," both by Vivian Shipley, appeared in *Perennial*, Negative Capability Press, Mobile, Alabama, 2015 and are printed here by permission of the author.

Maxine Susman: "Display of Kitchen Utensils" is printed here by permission of the author.

Susan Terris: "Mistress Melody Brown, 1898" first appeared in *Switched on Gutenberg*, 2016. This poem, along with "1887: Annie Oakley Is Done," is reprinted here by permission of the author.

Mary Langer Thompson: "My First Pink Slip" first appeared in *Eating Her Wedding Dress: A Collection of Clothing Poems*, Ragged Sky Press, Princeton, New Jersey, 2009, and is reprinted here by permission of the author.

Allison Thorpe: "I Award My Own Nobel Prize to Rosalind Franklin" is printed here by permission of the author.

Psyche Torok: "Remembrance" is printed here by permission of the author.

Karen Torop: "Meantime" is printed here by permission of the author.

Alison Townsend: "The Testimonial of Virginia Dare" is printed here by permission of the author.

Memye Curtis Tucker: "Seamstress" first appeared in *The Watchers*, © Memye Curtis Tucker, 1998. This material is used by permission of Ohio University Press, www.ohioswallow.com.

Index of Authors

CPSIA information can be obtained
at www.ICGtesting.com
Printed in the USA
FSHW04n2258230418
47186FS